Praise for *Your Inner GPS*

"Every once in a while a new teacher emerges, showing us a fresh way of looking at ourselves that can be truly transformational. With *Your Inner GPS*, Zen Cryar DeBrücke proves herself to be one of those teachers. She offers us a unique perspective and powerful tools that can change our lives."

— **Marci Shimoff,** #1 *New York Times*–bestselling author of
Happy for No Reason and *Chicken Soup for the Woman's Soul*

"Zen Cryar DeBrücke has created a masterpiece that explains your inner guidance and how to work with it to get the best results in your life. This book is definitely a must-read to understand your inner self better, to be happier, and to enjoy your life more."

— **Marie Diamond**, bestselling author of
The Energy Number Book

"Zen Cryar DeBrücke is a master who takes us by the hand and shows us that we all have deep wisdom within — our Internal Guidance System. Her book is filled with solid, doable instructions that can have a transformational effect on us, increasing joy in our lives. I couldn't recommend this book more highly."

— **Jack Canfield**, author of *The Success Principles*™ and
coauthor of the Chicken Soup for the Soul® series

"Our bodies often know more than our conscious minds. The world of gut feelings, hunches, and intuitions is so much easier to understand with Zen Cryar DeBrücke's Internal Guidance System. Both the techniques and the read itself feel like a breath of fresh air."

— **Robert Richman**, author of
The Culture Blueprint and former Zappos Culture Strategist

"Now more than ever, a planet in crisis needs humans who are willing and able to open up to, receive, and take inspired action on instructions from the unseen realms. As human consciousness evolves, many are courageous and willing, but few know how to tune in to and interpret spiritual guidance. This practical manual offers you accessible tools for empowering your intuition, your heart, and the Divine to guide your decisions. Ready to let the Divine take the lead in your life and to surrender yourself to being used as a secret agent of sacred service? If you're brave enough to say yes, get ready for magic, synchronicities, better health, more intimate relationships, a sense of meaning and purpose, and the deep fulfillment of knowing you are being used as a miracle worker on a planet where your love is much needed."

— **Lissa Rankin, MD**, founder of the Whole Health Medicine Institute and *New York Times*–bestselling author of *Mind Over Medicine* and *The Anatomy of a Calling*

"In *Your Inner GPS*, Zen Cryar DeBrücke provides a smart, direct, hands-on guide to transcend worry, fear, and stress to recharge, repurpose, and reconnect with your life's deepest meaning and purpose. Don't miss this one!"

— **JJ Virgin**, CNS, CHFS, celebrity nutrition and fitness expert and *New York Times*–bestselling author of *The Virgin Diet* and *The Sugar Impact Diet*

"Those ready to tap into their unlimited wisdom and supernatural powers can immediately put this book to use. Easy to read and fun to practice, *Your Inner GPS* will help many!"

— **Mike Dooley**, *New York Times*–bestselling author of *Infinite Possibilities* and *Leveraging the Universe*

"In *Your Inner GPS*, Zen Cryar DeBrücke provides a simple but powerful guidebook on how to use your own innate inner wisdom. This system, which you already have inside you, will transform anxiety, worry, and fear into confidence and joy. This book is filled with examples and exercises that quickly teach you how to follow your inner GPS daily. Fun to read and easy to do, the exercises will increase your confidence in making the right choices. Be prepared for success to materialize in all areas of your life."

— **Raymond Aaron**, bestselling author of
Double Your Income Doing What You Love

"Most of us have followed an inner voice that guided us to do something unexpected and led to a profound positive result. Zen Cryar DeBrücke shows us how to develop a daily relationship with this inner guidance. She shares a technology that has the potential to liberate us from habitual patterns, behaviors, thoughts, and emotions — a key to unlocking a direct experience of wholeness. Imagine living life to your full potential simply by discovering how to deeply listen to the always-present wise voice within that is your birthright. This book is a good guide."

— **Manju Lyn Bazzell**, keynote speaker and
former executive director of the Gangaji Foundation

"This book provides a step-by-step, easy-to-use process of using our own Internal Guidance System (IGS) to end needless suffering and create more happiness. Zen Cryar DeBrücke teaches us how to stop using dysfunctional thought patterns and how to be deliberate in using and trusting our IGS. I recommend DeBrücke's book and IGS courses."

— **Anita Sanchez**, PhD, coauthor of *Success University for Women*

"*Your Inner GPS* won't rock your world — these skills so warmly explored by the heart-master Zen Cryar DeBrücke will instead center your life as you navigate all kinds of compelling choices, daily chaos, and the unexpected that always drops in at the least fortuitous moment. In short, life as most of us know it can be buoyed by ongoing discovery and the clarity of this body intelligence that wakes up our inner wisdom and makes it both practical and profound. DeBrücke is the best friend/mentor to guide you in making sense of your inner landscape. You are going to love this book and use it every day."

— **Kathlyn Hendricks, PhD**, bestselling coauthor of
Conscious Loving and *Conscious Loving Ever After*

"In a world overpopulated by pundits, Zen Cryar DeBrücke's book is a breath of fresh air. This work guides you to a profound sense of self and self-trust. *Your Inner GPS* provides a set of practices for inner peace and a flight plan to freedom beyond the shackles of self-doubt."

— **Stewart Emery**, speaker, consultant,
and internationally bestselling author of *Actualizations*

"Zen Cryar DeBrücke has developed a brilliant yet simple way to listen to and interpret your inner guidance. Her ideas and exercises are profound, practical, and essential for living a successful and fulfilling life. This is a book to savor and digest."

— **Peggy Cappy**, author and creator of
Yoga for the Rest of Us, as seen on PBS

"We all have moments when we struggle and stress, and everything seems difficult. And then there are those times when the shoe fits perfectly, and just the faintest hint of action accomplishes miracles. The book you hold in your hand is the bridge between these two realities. Through accessing the Internal Guidance System you can tune your life in to what is simple and easy. I have tried what Zen Cryar DeBrücke writes about, and it works!"

— **Arjuna Ardagh**, founder of Awakening Coaching and
author of *Better Than Sex* and *The Translucent Revolution*

"If you have ever thought that some people seem to always make the right decisions, have awesome relationships, and generally appear happy, and you don't know why, then this book is for you. What sets them apart from others is their ability to lead their lives from the inside out and trust their inner GPS to effortlessly guide them to happiness and success. Zen Cryar DeBrücke gives you doable practices that work and a concrete how-to for listening to your Internal Guidance System and following its lead to greater happiness, fulfillment, and satisfaction in your life."

— **Natalie Ledwell**, cofounder of Mind Movies and
host of *The Inspiration Show*

YOUR INNER GPS

Follow Your Internal Guidance
to Optimal Health, Happiness, and Satisfaction

Zen Cryar DeBrücke

Foreword by Sonia Choquette

New World Library
Novato, California

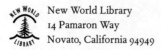 New World Library
14 Pamaron Way
Novato, California 94949

Cover images © Shutterstock
Text design by Tona Pearce Myers

Library of Congress Cataloging-in-Publication Data
Names: DeBrücke, Zen Cryar, date.
Title: Your inner GPS : follow your internal guidance to optimal health,
     happiness, and satisfaction / Zen Cryar DeBrücke.
Description: Novato, California : New World Library, [2016]
Identifiers: LCCN 2015051060 | ISBN 9781608684120 (paperback)
Subjects: LCSH: Intuition. | Insight. | Self-perception. | Mind and body. |
BISAC: BODY, MIND & SPIRIT / Inspiration & Personal Growth. | SELF-
     HELP / Personal Growth / Success. | BODY, MIND & SPIRIT / Parapsychology
     / ESP (Clairvoyance, Precognition, Telepathy). | SELF-HELP / Personal Growth
     / Happiness.
Classification: LCC BF315.5 .D43 2016 | DDC 158—dc23
LC record available at http://lccn.loc.gov/2015051060

First printing, May 2016
ISBN 978-1-60868-412-0
Ebook ISBN 978-1-60868-413-7
Printed in the USA on 100% postconsumer-waste recycled paper

 New World Library is proud to be a Gold Certified Environmentally
Responsible Publisher. Publisher certification awarded by Green Press
Initiative. www.greenpressinitiative.org

10   9   8   7   6   5   4   3   2   1

To my husband, Eric Cryar,
and my dear friend Bradley Rotter,
who have always had unwavering faith in me

Contents

PART TWO. Using Your IGS

PART THREE. Troubleshooting

Foreword

We, as a global society, are healing from a wounding that is the result of disconnection from our inner voice. I cannot imagine a more serious handicap with which to navigate through life. Fortunately, we are beginning to overcome the intellectual resistance to intuitive guidance that has been so prevalent in our culture. More and more people are recognizing that they feel lost, and that there is more to our being here, and our being guided, than meets the eye.

In *Your Inner GPS*, Zen DeBrücke so beautifully invites you to walk through easy-to-follow steps that will aid in your reconnection. This book provides reassurance that your Internal Guidance System is readily available and will work for you. It has been written with a genuine interest in your state of mind, as Zen invites you to give intuition a proper place in your life.

The benefit of tuning in to your inner guidance is that you begin to reclaim a sense of authenticity and personal empowerment. You can confidently trust the beautiful inner promptings that give voice and footing to your creative self, thereby liberating you from frustration or the inability to manifest the experiences held in your heart. Your IGS offers both a reconnection and a redirection, pulling us out of the past and the repeated tapes that keep us in self-doubt and confusion, and it opens the way for clear and receptive guided responses to people, to life, and to our dreams in present time.

Your intuition will show you the way to success while awakening your mojo, your life-inspired force, so that you can feel excitement while following the way. By honoring your Internal Guidance System, you awaken inner joy. It is a transformational experience that moves you beyond a state of being overwhelmed by disconnection, to one of becoming a part of something bigger than your defending ego. You will come to realize there are a lot of positive, loving allies available, both in this world and in other realms, and that life is truly wonderful.

The process of allowing your inner voice to lead you through life requires more than just a willingness to do so. When we are new to trusting ourselves, we need all the grounded guidance we can get. I have been blessed to be well supported in developing my intuition, and I have devoted my life to helping others do the same. I understand what it takes. For many years, I have known and personally witnessed Zen's authentic spirit and absolute dedication to empowering others. As you will discover, she is a clear and astute guide in the realm of subtle energy. That is why I wholeheartedly endorse this most practical and necessary book: her labor of love offers positive healing for all. She will be your grounded, clear, and competent ally in moving from resistance and confusion to joyful curiosity and clear inner direction. You can follow her direction with confidence as you rediscover what it is to live a satisfying life on your terms.

Sonia Choquette, author of *Ask Your Guides*

www.soniachoquette.com

was able to untangle any silly mess I got myself into and, at the same time, open doors I hadn't dreamed I could open.

In 1997, I followed the guidance of my IGS and left behind my work in exports. Instead, I started doing sales for an Internet hosting company. By 2000, I had become the CEO of a successful boutique Internet design firm in San Francisco. Then, in March 2000, the economy crashed. Fortunately, our firm was not affected by that first dot-com implosion — in large part because I'd followed the guidance of my IGS: We had transitioned our client base to almost solely *Fortune* 500 firms with solid capital and stability; we had no dot-com clients, only brick-and-mortar clients. I had also attempted to diversify our client base by opening an office in Europe. My intention was to move us away from the U.S.-based dot-com economy. However, I understood that we were still in a bubble that would eventually pop, and, sure enough, a few months later the stability of our clients turned out not to matter.

The second crash, in September 2001, was a shock wave felt around the world, and everyone cut back on spending and waited to see how bad things were going to be. When this occurred we had been expanding to keep up with the demand for our services. Suddenly my partners and I found ourselves with $1.2 million of personally secured debt.

Little did I know that my IGS was about to support me through one of the most challenging times of my life. I had followed it into this amazing industry and built a solid company with a great team — so what had happened? I decided that it had worked beautifully so far, and that now it was time to follow my IGS out of the situation and see how it stewarded me in times of deep fear and pain.

I am so happy that I did. My IGS kept me sane and even happy and confident during this trying period. In fact, I was so unusually calm that my friends, who were also experiencing the pain of the dot-com crash, began asking me to either give them the name of the doctor prescribing the drugs I was taking or tell them my secret. So I told them, "No drugs, but I do have a secret, and I call it my Internal Guidance System." From that moment on, I began to teach others about their IGSs, explaining how the system operates, how to interpret its guidance, and most important, how to remove the obstacles that our minds, the world, and our egos put in the way of following its guidance.

Let me share with you a few of the many ways I use my IGS. Mine transformed the way I experienced my past and my present, and it created my vision of the future. I found that when I mulled over old hurts from my childhood, whether the pain had been caused by family or friends, I could use my IGS to sense the actual truth of the situation — not simply how I had perceived it as a child, but what had happened from all perspectives involved.

My IGS helped me leave many painful memories behind forever, and my relationships transformed — which included healing my difficult relationship with my father. I was able to enjoy my time with my brother, too, even as I watched him get deathly sick and pass away. Every painful situation in my life that had left a mark began to be eased, and much of the pain was actually erased as new, open thoughts took the place of closed, suffering thoughts.

In my love relationships, my internal guidance brought me out of the destructive patterns I had repeated over and over again — the same old stuff, in each new relationship. Now that I had an internal compass that would react when I spoke negatively to my partners, I finally understood the part I had played in those ongoing sagas. I recognized that any attempts to manipulate and control my partners to get what I wanted would never ease my insecurities. The most amazing thing was that when these normally painful, negative aspects of my actions were revealed, it was not painful — it was a relief.

I felt compassionate about my own real and perceived faults, allowing me to better myself in an easy, even charmed way. My IGS was bringing me closer and closer to who I truly am inside when uncluttered by ego. It gave me the courage to set boundaries, speak my truth, and admit when I was wrong. The doubt I felt about what I should do in life went away, and I suddenly clearly understood how to communicate my needs and how to listen to the needs of others. There was this beautiful sensation of being comfortable in my own skin, and I gained a love and appreciation for myself, even when faced with my shadow side.

When your IGS shows you ugly things about yourself you don't want to see, it does so in a way that lets you feel wonderful and empowered. You feel confident that you can change what is not working, instead of remaining lost in the midst of the not-so-pleasant aspects of your ego.

The guidance it gives is down-to-earth and practical. For instance, on one occasion my IGS advised me not to book travel for a business trip. Then a week after I would have made my travel arrangements, I found out that the event was canceled, which meant I would have lost money on the airfare. I use my IGS to determine what to do and when to do it, and many times when I make a phone call, I hear the person say, "Amazing! I was just thinking about you this very moment." Once, I felt the urge to change plans that I'd made with a friend, and I later discovered that the friend ended up really needing to tend to her sick child. I felt ever so grateful that it all worked out so she could be at home.

My IGS manages my time and the sequence of how things are accomplished in my life. It controls what I call the flow — how my life literally flows along. Day after day I get so much done that it is mind-boggling. So much so that other people cannot figure out how I have done so much in my life. When the time is not right for something to be done, I can feel my IGS guiding me away from starting the task and pointing me to other tasks that are ready to be done. It is so cool to have what I need just as I need it, or just before I need it, for a particular task. The timing just works out that way. This alone has saved me thousands of dollars and countless hours of wasted effort. I see this as one of the most powerful unexplored business tools on the planet.

People often ask why so many seemingly magical, synergistic things happen to me. My answer is that when we get out of our own way, when we stop trying to force things, and when we follow the flow of this wise system called the IGS, synchronicity becomes the norm. In fact, I believe it is the way life normally works — the real way the world works — and that we have just gotten out of sync with it.

Now I am no longer alone in all these discoveries. Thousands of people are using their IGSs every day, getting the same results and feeling tremendous gratitude for this new way of living. Everyone has his or her very own IGS. You are born with it. It is looking out for you, just as mine is for me. I have never had so much joy and success in my life as I have had since committing to following and surrendering to the wise guidance and gentle nudging of my IGS.

I cannot tell you with absolute certainty how it knows all the things it does, or why it is so very accurate in providing me with the guidance I receive. I have a hunch, though. Given my life history, I feel it is the Holy Spirit. Others who are following their own IGSs have other conclusions that are just as accurate for them. I invite you to use it yourself and uncover what you think it is for you. Each student of the IGS gets their own impression of what this is, and I feel that is how it should be.

This journey is a personal and private one to be cherished and enjoyed. So begin your journey knowing that you will start seeing magical synergy in your life right away as this remarkable, natural, and innate guidance brings you greater health, happiness, and satisfaction. The best news is that you already have it; it is turned on and already working. Now, all you need to do is tap into it and start letting your own life flow.

How to Use This Book

This book is a manual that will support your ability to use your IGS to create health and happiness for years to come. For the past fifteen years, I have been teaching people from all over the world how to use their own. In that time I have discovered how to make learning to use the IGS easy and fun as it provides immediate results.

The book is divided into three parts, plus a conclusion. Part I gives you all the necessary general information about your Internal Guidance System: everything you need in order to understand how it operates. Part 2 helps you begin using your IGS every day. Your IGS is continually giving you guidance via sensations, and this part of the book will show you how to retrain your mind to tune in to those sensations and work with your IGS. That way you will begin to master it while you are completing the book. Part 3 is about troubleshooting, and I discuss the problems my students have faced when using their IGSs. I outline various hiccups that can happen and recommend solutions. Finally, the conclusion provides you with a bit of inspiration and gives you perspective on how using your IGS can beautifully transform our world.

Throughout the book, you'll find practices that will help you access and engage your IGS. There are two types of practices: some that teach you how to use your IGS, and others that you turn to when you cannot get answers or properly feel your IGS. Each practice contributes to a new awareness of your mind and your body. This is similar to working a muscle. It takes repetition over time, which is why we call them practices — you need to practice them to get the results! Once you have used each for a week or so, either repeat the process — performing one practice per week again — or simply use the practices whenever you feel you need them.

The first practice, the listening meditation in part 1 (see page 18), lays the foundation for success. It can help you quickly and easily get into a clear mental space before you try to use your IGS. I highly recommend that you return to it — or the expanded version, "Deepening Your Listening Practice" in part 2 (see page 64) — often.

I suggest you do the practices in part 2 in the order in which they are given. They will support you in getting accurate guidance that you can use as a normal, everyday part of your life. The order is important because, when you do them in order, they will feel easy. If you do them out of order the process may feel much more challenging than it is. Most people who experience pitfalls when beginning to use their IGS do so because they don't do the practices in order and they don't do each of them long enough.

However, if you get stuck doing the practices in part 2 and feel like they're harder than they should be, I invite you to simply move ahead to those in part 3, the troubleshooting portion of the book. The practices in part 3 are there to support you in using your IGS when it feels hard or you feel stuck in some way. Uncover what's happening between you, your IGS, and your mind by trying the practice associated with what you are experiencing. This way you can get unstuck quickly and return to the practices in part 2.

Enjoy the practices. They are interesting and fun. You're getting to know a new part of yourself, and you'll be pleasantly surprised at how easy life becomes when you follow your IGS.

PART ONE

YOUR IGS

What It Is, How It Works,
and Why It's Important

What Is Your IGS?

You were born with a factory-installed guidance system. It is like the GPS in a car. This system is called your Internal Guidance System, or IGS.

The guidance it gives you has many different purposes. The most important one is to get you from one end of your life to the other with as much joy, ease, and fulfillment as possible. Throughout the book, I will reveal other parts of its purpose in guiding you. For now it is important for you to recognize that it knows and deeply understands everything you desire to achieve, as well as countless things you have yet to even think of. It also knows specifically *how* you would most like for your desires to be achieved. Its purpose is to guide you to the specific way of going about your life that will make you, and everyone around you, the happiest.

The reason its guidance is unique and special is because it was designed just for you and your life purposes. What I have discovered is that we have not just one life purpose but several, if not hundreds of them: to be a good parent, to support particular people in our lives, to be a good child, to care for aging parents, to transform the world around us in either little or big ways. Your life purposes can range from something as simple as giving the perfect book to someone at just the right time, to transforming the industry you work in, to giving your child the start in life they need to accomplish their own life's purposes.

There are also things in your life that are not yours to do, and your IGS will guide you away from them so you don't waste your life force or use it unsuccessfully. As a group these purposes can feel overwhelming, but with your IGS it is not only possible but also easy and enjoyable to do it all.

This inner GPS contains your life's specific road map, which shows on a soul level all the things you are here to participate in, experience, and achieve. Your GPS is with you every moment of every day, constantly there to support you — to give you guidance about what you are thinking and doing and how you are being. This can sound a bit scary or uncomfortable, until you realize that it has no judgment on any of these aspects. It does not think of you as good or bad. It relates to you as a soul that it is here to guide and protect. It knows who you really are deep down inside. It knows the "pre-you," the one who preceded who you are now. One of its purposes is to help you uncover and remember who you really are — the "you" who existed before life took over and covered up your perfection and beauty. It has only unconditional love for you and the journey you are on.

Your IGS is very much like a wise best friend, a career counselor, a life coach, and a spiritual teacher all rolled into one. In fact, it is so amazing and interesting that I had to write an entire book to introduce you to it.

How Your IGS Works

Your IGS provides guidance by giving you sensations in your body. It resides in the area between your throat and solar plexus. The solar plexus is the triangular area between your lower ribs, above your stomach. The sensations that you feel in this area of your body are forms of guidance.

As you are thinking, your IGS is listening and sending a physical signal letting you know whether your thoughts are true, aligned with your purpose, and taking you toward health and happiness.

Your IGS creates what I like to call an *urging feeling*. It nudges you to move toward various activities in the world around you. It feels like a desire upwelling inside you. For an example, think of the last time you had an urge to call a friend or family member. When you followed that urge, did they respond with "I was just thinking of you!" or possibly "I really needed to talk to you. How did you know?" That urge was from your IGS.

Your IGS provides you with information that supports you as you:

- respond to your life as it develops instead of reacting to it according to false scenarios, old habits, or unconscious beliefs; and
- learn to focus on your desires instead of fears.

By learning to follow your IGS, you will find that your life seems to work out, that it is somehow just right in the way it unfolds, and that you become a magnet for what many consider small and large miracles. Now it is time to give you an experience of how it feels to receive guidance from your IGS.

How to Quiet Your Mind to Feel Your IGS

First, it is important to get yourself relaxed, to center yourself, and to feel your body. It may seem silly to think that you are not feeling your body, but very often we go through life in our minds. By that, I mean we focus on our thoughts instead of on the world around us or on what our bodies are experiencing. Have you ever driven home and found that you don't remember actually driving home? What about finding a mysterious bruise on your leg and realizing you don't remember how it got there? These are examples of times when you were not feeling your body.

Since your IGS communicates with you through sensations located between the throat and solar plexus, it is important to start by making sure you are connecting to what your body is feeling. Below is a simple practice that will make it easier for you to consciously experience your IGS for the first time — or, as I call it, "drop into your listening."

When I coach people to use their IGS, I tell them, "Drop into your listening." I recommend you do this easy practice whenever you want to interpret guidance from your IGS. I will be giving you a more advanced practice shortly to help you deepen this listening practice. For now, I want you to quiet your mind so we can move to the next practice, feeling your IGS. First read through the practice, and then do it for a minute or two before you go on to the next section.

PRACTICE

Sit up straight with both feet on the floor and your hands resting in your lap. Close your eyes and take a deep breath, slowly letting it out. As you do, start focusing on relaxing from head to toe, relaxing your body as your awareness moves downward from your head to your torso, down into your legs, and to your feet.

Next, stop and focus on what the bottoms of your feet feel like as they rest on the floor. Really take the time to feel your feet. They may suddenly come alive as you put your attention on them, becoming slightly tingly. Take a moment and feel your toes, from your big toes to your little toes, now the arches of your feet, then finally the heels. Experience the pressure between your toes and heels. Relax, breathe deeply, and stay focused on your feet as you also feel the force of gravity gently helping you sink more deeply into your chair.

Now, shift your awareness to the palms of your hands resting in your lap.

Feel your palms come alive and tingle slightly as you become more aware of them. Stay focused on both your feet and your hands at the same time.

While staying focused on your feet and hands, begin to listen to the room around you.

What are you hearing? Try to listen to the sounds of the

room around you without letting your mind name the sounds. If your mind begins to think "bird, car, fan, talking," then focus on your feet and hands and listen again. Just *be* with the sounds you hear in the room in the same way you are *being* with your feet and hands. As you focus on hearing, try not to judge or name what you are hearing. Instead, just experience the sounds. Practice that for a minute or two before moving on. It is very important and will greatly help you feel your IGS. Remember: *feet, hands, then listening.* It is not a problem if your mind begins to wander. Simply return to feeling your feet and your hands and to listening to the room around you.

Now, why am I having you do this? When you focus on more than one body sensation at a time, your mind begins to quiet. It may seem complex at first, but very quickly, with a small amount of practice, you will be able to do it in a second without anyone noticing. What this will do is allow you to move from your mind to your IGS in a moment so you can interpret the guidance you are receiving.

Please don't be frustrated if at first it takes a minute or two to drop into your listening — especially if you are new to mind-quieting practices, or if you are not used to relaxing the mind by focusing on three body sensations at once. Let yourself take the time you need to really listen, releasing your mind from thinking. If at any time during the meditation you find your mind becoming active again, just relax and notice your feet on the floor, notice your hands, and go back to listening to what is both near and far away.

A Simple Meditation to Feel Your IGS

Before you do this meditation, put away anything that is distracting, and find a quiet area. Sit down and relax. It can be very helpful to close your eyes. Start by focusing on the sensations in your feet and hands. Then bring your awareness into your chest area, drop into your listening, and think the following statement:

I do not have an Internal Guidance System.

Try to let the statement pass quietly and slowly through your mind. Try not to hold on to the thought or concentrate on it at all. Instead, simply imagine the statement floating through your mind as if it were a cloud passing through the sky. If your mind reacts to the statement, just let that thought go and put your focus back on your feet and hands and what you are hearing in the room around you. You might want to repeat the statement again out loud. When you think or say the thought to yourself, notice the first sensation you feel in the area between your throat and stomach. If you feel something, describe it to yourself out loud in words or write it down on a piece of paper.

When you've noted your sensation, move on and try the statement below in the same way. Notice what you are hearing, without naming or judging the sounds. Relax, keep your eyes closed, and when your mind quiets, drop into your listening and think the following statement, seeing the thought as a cloud passing through the sky of your mind:

I do have an Internal Guidance System.

Again, notice the first sensation you feel between your throat and stomach area. Describe it to yourself out loud or write it down. It could be a strong feeling or a subtle one. If you have no sensation at all, don't be concerned. This is a normal response when first becoming aware of your IGS. Focus again on how your hands and feet feel, putting your attention on the practice of listening in order to quiet your mind one more time before moving on.

If you had trouble or did not notice anything, please go to www.yourinnergps.org/feel_it and view the video there, which will guide you through the process. It may be easier than the above practice. You can always go back later and follow the above instructions on your own.

What Did You Feel?

What you may have felt in the meditation are sensations of expansion/opening and contraction/closing in your chest, throat, and/or solar plexus area.

Very often when people state, "I do not have an Internal Guidance System," they report feeling a tightening, a constriction, a pressure in their chest, or a feeling of being less able to breathe. For some, it feels like a "dropping" or a "wilting." Others realize they have felt the sensation of constriction before and called it a feeling of anxiety, stress, or worry. This is the sensation I refer to throughout the book as "closing" or "being closed."

Often when people state, "I do have an Internal Guidance System," they notice that their chest seems to "open up." Some describe it as an expansion, a release of pressure, a relaxing feeling, an upward opening of energy rising in a V or Y shape, a sense of lightness or an ability to breathe more deeply. This is what I refer to as "opening" or "being open" throughout the book. If you felt none of these things, don't worry. Your IGS is there, and you will begin to realize what it is as you read a bit further.

Some people (often because of their careers) have to live in their minds — strategizing, planning, and creating all the time. If this is true for you, you may be so used to not feeling the sensations your body produces — such as hunger, thirst, tiredness, or even stress — that it can take a bit more practice, by dropping into your listening, to get in touch with your IGS. You may want to spend more time focusing on feeling your body to make it easier for you to recognize the sensations of your IGS.

The practices in this book will support you in naturally connecting your IGS to your thoughts. What I can tell you is that you have been feeling your IGS all your life but, most likely, have been identifying the sensation of closing as stress, fear, and anxiety, and the sensation of opening as desire, passion, and confidence. So just read on, and in no time you will be delighted to discover you are easily feeling and receiving the insightful guidance of your IGS. The first practice in part 2 will deepen the experience of "dropping into your listening," which will help you feel your body more clearly and, as a result, your IGS. Feel free to skip ahead to page 64 and try it out. You will need to do it for a few days, while doing different activities, so getting started is a good idea.

Why Is It Important to Follow Your IGS?

Your IGS is more than just a guidance system for your life's purpose. Another aspect of what it does is reprogram the thoughts in your mind that are false and limiting and that come from your past, not your present experiences. Let me give you an example of this. I apologize in advance for using a North America–centric example, but I think you will get the point. For years I have been teaching people how to use the IGS. In my course, I ask people from the United States and even Canada: "What color is a yield sign?" and 85 to 90 percent of the participants answer "yellow and black."

This answer is actually incorrect. The colors of a yield sign in the United States are red and white. In fact even when I tell people this, they still cannot recall a yield sign that is red and white; some even vehemently tell me they will take a picture of one and send it to me. To date, no photos have arrived of a yellow-and-black yield sign.

An interesting test of this is to ask random people from the United States what color a yield sign is and get a sense of this for yourself. Here is an astonishing fact: If you answer "yellow and black," even though you have been given the correct answer you will not remember "red and white" in two months' time. What? That's right. My giving you the answer did not update your mind's opinion about the color of yield signs in the United States. You cannot simply update your mind by adding new information. Updating has to be done through the nervous system.

If I gave you a box of crayons, showed you a picture of a red-and-white yield sign, and asked you to draw it, then you could remember that it was red. One of the ways your mind is programmed for permanent retention of information is through your nervous system, which is what your IGS uses to guide you. The mind does not respond well to new information that comes in once. It will revert back to old habits unless you physically make an effort (by using flash cards, swinging a racket, driving, or engaging in any other repetitive practice) to create new mental, "muscle" memory.

In 1971 the yield sign changed from yellow and black to red and white. There have been no yellow yield signs for forty-five years. Just a few months ago I was watching a brand-new episode of *Sesame Street*, a children's program in the United States, in which they displayed a yellow yield sign in one of their skits. Now my son, who was sixteen months old at the time, has seen and experienced the yellow yield sign. That is how the information continues long after the sign has been retired. Now, why are people still using the yellow yield sign?

At birth, our minds are sponges, taking in new information to help us grow and survive. Our minds, without our help, notice everything around us and absorb the experiences and details at an extraordinary rate. Then, as we get older, our minds gradually slow down. Our minds do not have a way to update the information they receive during this time. They do not one day suddenly see a red-and-white yield sign and say, "Hey, that changed, so I need to update that information." The yellow yield sign prevails because it is still being used in advertising, on book covers, in television programs, and in other strange ways you would never expect.

I was in a leadership course a few years ago where we all had to form teams and do a presentation. One group decided to do "Yield before you speak" as their topic. When we came to their room for the presentation, there were over a hundred handmade yellow yield signs hanging from the ceiling and the walls and on the tables. I did not feel the need to correct them, since their point was made, and most likely only 10–15 percent of the audience knew the difference anyway. It does go to show that even though we pass thousands of red-and-white yield signs every year, we still can be completely unaware of what a yield sign really looks like.

The importance of this is that, for every area of our lives, our minds are recalling the equivalents of those outdated yellow signs. They are everywhere: relationships, emotions, careers, our body image, what we believe we can do or can't do, the success of our household, community, government, and the planet. In relation to these things, the outdated information that we're still holding on to creates limitations in our lives that are taking us away from achieving our hearts' desires. All the hidden, outdated "yellow yield signs" in our lives are stopping our creativity, keeping us from knowing what is possible, and preventing us from creating health in our minds, bodies, and spirits. Stop for one moment and think. If you have an unexamined thought that is keeping you from all your happiness, wouldn't you want to know about it?

Your IGS knows about your personal outdated yellow yield signs, and by using the openings and closings as guidance it shows you that they are there. It supports you via closing sensations that prompt you to question the thoughts your mind is producing. That way you can know what needs to be updated or improved. Not only that, but when you have an opening sensation, it occurs via your nervous system, which reprograms your mind and locks in the new thoughts, eventually replacing the thoughts that are old and outdated.

The more you use your IGS, the more you turn the guidance that results in a closing sensation into thoughts that produce the sensation of opening — and the more you recalibrate your mind to make use of what is present and real in this moment. In working with students, I observe a powerful aspect of the IGS, one that amazes me. No matter how deep or powerful a thought, emotion, or belief is for a person, once they find the truth by means of the opening sensation produced by their IGS, they can no longer believe the untrue thought. They feel the truth in their deepest being and, in doing so, create a vibrant new path.

As you do the practices described in this book, you will begin to experience this process for yourself. The more you attune yourself to the thoughts that open you, the more you leave behind the ones that close you, and the more you clear out what is not working in your life. It is a natural outcome of finding openings.

What Is Stress?

Stress is a strange aspect of being human. Researchers who study stress understand what it does, but they don't truly know what stress is. They know the effects that long-term stress has on the brain: it shrinks your brain — it literally shrinks it, causing memory loss, loss of clarity, loss of creative thinking, and the destruction of specific neural pathways. It begins to collapse your capacity to think critically. Prolonged stress on the body creates heart issues, constricted blood vessels, bowel problems, sleep problems, depression, and anxiety. In fact, stress is linked to all six of the leading causes of death in the United States. Even cancer has been linked to stress.

As I noted, researchers do not *know* what stress is. I believe the reason why is because it is different for each person. You have a specific set of stress factors that are unique to you. What stresses you may not stress me. You may notice this in the people around you, including your significant other. My husband and I, for example, have very different stress triggers. In addition, the way stress affects your body may not be the way it affects my body. So, there's no one way that we can all handle or manage stress.

Now researchers have discovered that we can become addicted to stress. We find ourselves living in this modern world where we are overwhelmed, constantly mentally turned on, plugged in, overworked, and so overrun with tasks that some of us can't seem to live comfortably without the stress. Without stress, some people report not knowing how to be and how to relax. How is this happening?

Our bodies fight stress by triggering hormones in an attempt to balance out the effects of the stress. These hormones are adrenaline, cortisol, and norepinephrine. Too much cortisol can suppress the immune system, decrease libido, increase blood pressure and sugar levels, and contribute to obesity and many more unhealthy conditions in the body. Under constant stress, our bodies get used to these hormones, especially the high cortisol levels — and our bodies can begin to crave them, believing they need them to survive. As a result, we begin to add stress to our lives instead of extracting it. We no longer know how to de-stress. The body gets to a place where it just bounces back and forth between a state of some stress and a state of lots of stress, and it never gets to an unstressed state. No matter what a person under these conditions tries to do — meditation, exercise, extra sleep, reading a book, or gardening — their stress level never quite gets back to that healthy place they were in when they were younger.

I want to introduce you to a new way of thinking about this. Stress comes almost solely from your mind. Yes, you can feel physically stressed when your IGS is in the contracted, closed state. I believe this state is actually the foundation of what stress in the body is. Stress is produced by the mind when your thoughts are out of alignment, untrue, and not moving you toward happiness and success. When your IGS is expanded, it reverses the effects of being closed (that is, the effects of stress) on your body. When it's open, it supports good health, mental clarity, and overall well-being.

It is your thoughts that create both the sense of contraction (stress) and the sense of expansion (relaxation). Your IGS is in charge of letting you know where you are in this cycle at any given moment. One of its purposes is to help you fully relax. How great that you have an inner GPS moving you toward being relaxed in life! When you feel an opening sensation in response to what you are thinking, you begin to reprogram your mind and remove the effects of the stress hormones. You then program yourself to maintain a stress-free environment mentally. Using your IGS is one of the healthiest things you can do for your body. It creates a healthy inner state of being that generates not only happiness but also good health.

What Causes Anxiety and Worry?

Anxiety and worry are essentially the same thing. Worry is the little sister of anxiety, but the sensations and reasons for them are the same. These are the sensations you feel when you are unclear about how something will turn out and you fear that it will turn out badly. Everyone experiences times of worry and anxiety, whether before taking a test, going to a big meeting at work, speaking in front of others, or making an important decision. I'd like to offer a new way of looking at these two sensations: as guidance from your IGS. This guidance can be as subtle as a slightly uncomfortable feeling in your chest or as overpowering as the sensation of a panic attack. The stronger the sensation, the more untrue and out of alignment your thoughts are about what could happen or is happening.

As you learn to use and trust your IGS, you begin to worry less and feel less anxious about uncertainties in your life. The reason is that you realize your IGS knows your future. Yes, I understand this sounds a bit crazy, but it is the truth. Time and again in my own life and in my clients' lives, I have been surprised at how accurately the IGS understands how situations will unfold. So when an uncertain or fearful possible future comes to mind, your IGS will close if that future is not going to happen and open if it is. Then all you have to do is simply focus your thoughts elsewhere and stop the mental chatter associated with worry and anxiety.

Also, please know that continuing to focus your thinking in the wrong direction is fruitless and a waste of your life force. It is also unhealthy. Your IGS uses your nervous system to send you guiding sensations. This system was never meant to be so overtaxed. In our recent past, life was so much simpler. As life gets more complex and fast-paced, so does our need to re-focus our thoughts on openings so we can retain our health. The pressure caused by all the decisions we need to make and all the tasks we have to accomplish can create too much tension in our bodies if we don't know how to find openings. The IGS, when used properly, promotes equilibrium in our lives.

A few of my clients have believed that if they worried enough, they could prevent bad things from happening. This is actually the opposite of what is true. By focusing on thoughts that create a closing sensation, you are more likely to miss key things that will bring you out of the situation you are in. The best way to prevent bad things from happening is to use your IGS to get clear directions on what you do need to do to move toward success and away from a future that you fear.

The sensations of worry and anxiety are an alarm going off to let you know that it is time to look closer at what you are thinking of doing or what you think will happen. Recognize instead that your worries are not true, and then look for an opening sensation created by your IGS. The practices in part 2 will walk you through this. For now, begin to think of worry and anxiety as closing sensations that come from your IGS, which is responding to thoughts your mind is producing about things that are not going to happen. Your mind is trying to warn you about real problems it thinks are going to happen based on what has happened in your past, not what is actually going to happen now or in the future.

Fear: Desire Unexpressed

We can define fear as an unpleasant thought or emotion caused by a perceived threat. The mind is often on the lookout for threats to your survival or your happiness or for something that will cause you pain. The challenge once again is that your mind can perceive threats where there are none. One of my favorite acronyms for fear is "false evidence appearing real." This so clearly describes the relationship between your IGS and the mind's fears.

What I have discovered about most of our fears is that they are actually desires that are going unexpressed in our bodies. When our minds generate fear, they are operating from a place of a desire that we have forgotten or are unaware that we have. Each of us, from the time we are born, are meant to explore our desires and produce our lives from our heart's deepest desires. Along the way, we get disconnected from our desires and slowly begin to leave them behind. We leave them behind for many reasons: we are told they are childish, that we cannot have those desires, that we are not good enough to have those desires, or that they are just impossible for a person such as ourselves to attain.

Your IGS is always in touch with your desires and is working to reawaken you to the desires you have inside. Until you reawaken to them, you may find that they show up as fear. Fear is a path back to remembering your heart's deepest desires. As we grow up and grow older, we come to believe that we can achieve only certain desires. As we give up on some of our desires, we build a reservoir of fear. The fastest way to release fear is to discover the desire that we have locked away inside us.

Let me clarify what I mean by *desire*. I don't mean the type of desire we have for the things that we use in order to feel better and that can turn into addictions — such as chocolate, sex, sugar, tobacco, prescription or nonprescription drugs, or anything else that we use to alter the feeling of being less than satisfied and happy with life. I am talking about desires that come from the deepest parts of our heart and soul.

Fear is most often a sensation of closing produced by the IGS. There are also fears that will open you, and they are very real. If you sense an opening in response to a thought that frightens you, then you need to take action, for that is no longer just a fear but a reality. Years ago I was having a challenging time financially. I was living hand-to-mouth, month after month. One of my biggest fears was not having enough money to pay my rent. Month after month I felt a closing sensation at the thought of not having my rent, and an opening sensation that indicated the funds would be there. During one particularly difficult month, I was thinking again that I would not have enough money for rent. All of a sudden I realized that this thought opened me! Boy, that was such a shock, because usually I closed at thoughts like that. I asked my IGS if my landlord was going to evict me, and I closed. Then I asked if it would cause problems between my landlord and me. Again I closed. At the time I lived in a duplex and my landlord lived in the other unit. I asked if I needed to proactively go to my landlord right away and let him know, and I opened. So off I went to have a challenging conversation, but I was open about it. It went great. He was wonderful about it; I caught up in about three months and all was well.

Fear can cause either an opening or a closing sensation, but most often it is the latter. When you are afraid of something, notice how your IGS is feeling — look mostly for sensations in your chest and solar plexus. If you are closed, that fear is not going to happen. If you are open, inquire further to find out what needs to happen next.

If you find that you are a fearful person in general, that your stress often comes in the form of fear, then you have desires that you are not expressing. Not asking for what you truly desire turns into fear in the body and can fill you up so that it is difficult to not feel fear most of the time. I have supported clients in moving through this situation, and it is actually fun and simple. Do the fear practice on page 118. Do it often — as often as you feel fear. You will find that you can empty yourself of fear and have a new practice to keep yourself filled with desire instead.

Fear, anxiety, worry, and stress are all alarms going off, asking you to check your thoughts, find the ones that give you a sense of closing, and turn them into thoughts that open you. You can use the practices in this book to find openings and focus on them instead. The reason I have defined and discussed these four emotions that prompt a sense of closing is that they are the basis of many of the equivalents of the obsolete yellow yield signs of our lives. We need a way to become aware of our blind spots that are holding us back from true happiness and even joy. By becoming aware of them, you will be well on your way to clearing away the false thoughts and moving into what is true for you and your life.

Neutral Is One of the Guiding Sensations

Not feeling anything may simply be guidance that takes the form of a "neutral" sensation, which is still information from your IGS. The IGS generates three types of sensations in varying degrees — opening, closing, *and* neutral — and it is important to note that each sensation can carry a different level of intensity.

Sometimes when people are having trouble feeling their IGSs, it is because they have a preconceived notion of what the experience should feel like. The mind looks for what *it thinks* the IGS is going to feel like, which can block out what is actually being felt. That is another example of being in your mind instead of being in your body. The solution to this is to continue to explore what you are thinking and how your body is feeling, and not to worry about the neutral sensations. You will feel your closings and can begin to explore your IGS from there. The previous exercise, where I used the sentences "I do have..." and "I do not have an Internal Guidance System" so that you could feel your IGS, was designed just to let you start feeling it. It works for most people, but not everyone.

If you don't feel it, you may be trying to focus on the single statement in the meditation while your mind is actually generating many thoughts, such as: "Is that it? What does that mean? I do not have an Internal Guidance System. Of course I have a guidance system. Am I still feeling my feet?" This is not focusing on one thought, and your IGS tries to respond to all thoughts that you are thinking. If you are generating too many conflicting thoughts, you may feel a neutral sensation. This is meant to guide you to slow your thinking down so your IGS can give you guidance more effectively. It can take practice to think just one thought. As you read further I will give you lots of ways to begin recognizing the sensations of your IGS. The best way I have found is to do the listening practice and become adept at "dropping into your listening" when you want to explore your thoughts using your IGS.

Think of Your IGS as a Compass, Not a Yes-or-No System

One of the first conclusions that people come to is that the IGS operates as a "yes" or a "no." They assume that if you feel closed, that is a no, and if you feel open you are getting a yes. This is not how it operates. Your IGS is closer to a compass that is used to navigate the planet.

A compass, when guiding you northward, is always moving slightly back and forth. This is because true magnetic north fluctuates. Your IGS is always fluctuating too — creating opening and closing sensations, always slightly shifting as what you are thinking shifts. It is highly attuned to where the focus of your thoughts is leading you.

Picture, for a moment, just half of a compass: north represents your greatest joy, west represents the neutral zone, and south represents your most terrifying sensations of panic and despair. Your IGS will give you sensations from one end of this spectrum to the other, all based on whether your thoughts are moving you forward into a fulfilled life or away from it. Think of your IGS as the needle on the compass, which has many different points: south — panic; southwest — anxiety; west

— calmness; northwest — happiness and peace; north — joy. Of course, there are many different degrees of these sensations that you will feel as the needle ranges from the south point to the north point, and each gives you the degree of fulfillment or lack of fulfillment that you are moving toward.

It is important to note that these are not emotions. Rather, they are what the sensations generated by your IGS often feel like when they are experienced. Later we will discuss the difference between emotional energy and the sensations your IGS gives you.

Here's another way to think about the guidance from your IGS: experiencing it is similar to the "hot or cold" game we played as children, where one child is blindfolded and the others try to guide the blindfolded child toward the prize using the terms *cold*, *colder*, *warm*, *warmer*, *hot*, and *hottest*. Your IGS, however, uses varying levels of opening, neutral, and closing sensations. The more clearly you feel that expanded, opening energy, the more your thoughts are moving you in a successful direction. The more clearly you feel closed sensations like worry, fear, stress, and panic, the farther away your thoughts are carrying you from having success.

The Anatomy of Your IGS

Your IGS produces the sensations of guidance in three areas of your body: throat, chest, and solar plexus. When you feel sensations in these areas, you are having thoughts that fall into three categories:

1. Disempowering yourself personally.
2. Real-time information regarding thoughts you are having about actions to take or that you have taken.
3. Beliefs of yours that are preventing you from moving toward success and fulfillment.

Let's look at each of those physical areas in detail.

Throat

Have you ever felt a tightening or a closing in your throat? It can almost feel as if you have something lodged in your throat, or as if you cannot swallow. This is guidance from your IGS. It means the thoughts you are having about yourself at that moment are limiting you, preventing you from undertaking what you are truly capable of; they are not empowering you to achieve success in the situation you are in. Very often the emotion of shame or embarrassment accompanies this closing sensation. The throat area does not have the corresponding opening sensation that the chest does. In fact, the throat is open most of the time, closing only when the thoughts mentioned above are present.

Examples of such thoughts are:

- He/she really doesn't love me, understand me, or care about me.
- I have failed again. I will never get ahead in life, this job, or this relationship.
- I can't say what I really feel, think, or believe, because I will be hurt, rejected, or attacked.
- I sound stupid, ridiculous, embarrassing, or ignorant.

If you feel a closing in your throat area, check your thoughts about who you are or how you think you are being perceived by others in the situation. When you identify the thoughts, you will find they are about your not having power. Your IGS is letting you know that these thoughts are *not true, that this is not how others perceive you*, and that these thoughts are not guiding you to happiness and success. Practices in part 2 will help you shift to thoughts that create a release of the throat into a more open state.

Chest

When your chest is experiencing the opening sensation, it can feel as slight as a hint of relaxation or as strong as a rush of expanding energy, depending on how on-target your thoughts are as they move you toward success and happiness. When your chest is experiencing the closing sensation, it can feel slightly tight or as if you're having a panic attack, depending on how far away the thoughts are taking you from being successful and happy.

The sensations in your chest correspond to what you are thinking about the past, the current moment, or the future. This area of the IGS is what you will likely feel most often, and it provides effective guidance throughout your normal day.

Examples of these thoughts are:

- I should do the grocery shopping after work today. (Open or closed?)
- My new client seems to be wavering; maybe I should offer them something as an incentive. (Open or closed?)
- I have not heard back from my friend regarding attending our party. Did I do something to upset her? (Open or closed?)

Sensations in your chest are giving you guidance on everyday living. As you go about your life, become aware of this area of your body and it will guide you toward being more at ease and in the flow. Practices in part 2 will begin to help you build your awareness and understanding of this type of guidance.

Solar Plexus

The guidance you receive in this area from your IGS is life-changing. Closing sensations in the solar plexus feel like an upset stomach, as if there is a rock or a churning tightness where your ribs come together. You may find that the sensation is constant; it does not expand and contract like a sensation in your chest area does. As you move about your day, no matter what you are thinking, doing, or feeling, it is still there. When this area is closed, the sensation does not come and go and, in fact, can become a background sensation, one that you may not be aware of unless you slow down. There is no corresponding opening sensation in this area. If you are open in the solar plexus you will not notice anything at all.

The importance of this area is that it informs you of a belief system — or what we can refer to as a *body of thought* — that colors how you think about something. This is the area that often uncovers the equivalents of those mistakenly remembered yellow yield signs in your mind that are holding you back from happiness and satisfaction. This is when you have one large, all-informing idea that is *not* true about yourself, your life, or how the world works. This body of thought is keeping you from the true perspective that will lead you to success and happiness.

Examples of this include:

- I have lost my job and will not be able to find another one.
- My spouse does not respect and appreciate me.
- I am unhealthy, and I am not ever going to be healthy.
- The manager of the department has it in for me. No matter what I do they will not let me get ahead.

These may not seem like thoughts that you hold. I have broken them down to their simplest forms. For example, in your relationship, you might have the thought that your partner can never tell you often enough that he or she loves you. Everything that he or she does is attributed to not loving you or to not being sufficiently supportive of you. When this happens, your mind brings to the forefront all kinds of past and present

situations that it uses to prove that this body of thought is accurate. Your solar plexus closes and stays that way as long as
you are generating that story. In part 2, there's information on
how to shift this.

Another aspect of guidance generated within your solar
plexus becomes evident when you experience a life-changing
event: losing your job, getting a divorce, or some other situation that can dramatically affect your future. All your thoughts
begin to revolve around the new projected future. For example,
you lose your job, and then all you can think about is how much
money you have to survive on, what you are no longer able to
afford, or your fears about how you are going to keep up the
lifestyle to which you have become accustomed. You may find
yourself turning down offers to do things with friends, looking
in the grocery store for the cheapest items, or cutting out things
that are not necessarily what you should be sacrificing.

This overwhelming body of thought may take over every
aspect of your life. This is when your IGS will send guidance
in the form of a closing sensation in your solar plexus that will
stay until you stop thinking that way. It does this so that you
can become aware that these thoughts are *not* bringing you
closer to greater fulfillment and are possibly creating what
you do not want more of in your life. If cutting costs and being
aware of the possible savings are in order, you will feel empowered and open as you make these choices. Your IGS will always
provide you with a sense of ease and satisfaction when what
you are choosing is truly leading you toward more success in
any situation.

Your IGS Closing Is Always about What You Are Thinking

When I first began my attempt to understand the sensations from my IGS, I found that the most challenging thing to remember was that the guidance related only to what I was thinking. When I felt an opening sensation, it was about the thoughts I was having, and when I felt a closing sensation, it was about the thoughts I was having. This is a dramatic shift from my belief that others and the world around me were the cause of my feeling bad or good. You may need to constantly remind yourself to change how you are thinking about something or someone.

Every person I have ever taught to use their IGS has believed that when they felt a closing sensation (i.e., anxiety, worry, or fear), something bad was about to happen, that the person they were thinking about was the problem, or that what they were thinking about was going to come true. This is false! Here's the way it works: when you get a closing sensation, it means that *what you are thinking* is not going to happen, is not the truth, is not accurate, and is not leading you toward success, and that your thinking about it is wrong, out of alignment. It is up to you to find where your thinking about this person or thing needs to be corrected.

Let's say you get a phone call from a client. They are rushed and sound abrupt, and they cancel an appointment with you. You begin to think maybe they are unhappy with you. Possibly your mind brings up fears you have about your work or product and then attributes this to the action your client just took. Most often in these situations you will get a corresponding sensation of tightness in your IGS. Let's say it is in your solar plexus. All of our lives, we have had these feelings, and since we actually physically feel what we perceive as uncomfortable sensations (IGS guidance), we assume that it is because the client *is* unhappy with us, and that somehow a part of us knows this and is warning us. When working with your IGS, the most challenging aspect in the beginning is to remember that the closing feeling means your thoughts *are not true*, and that they are leading you away from a happy outcome. What if you were to continue down the same thought path, that your client is unhappy? What would you do? Call them and try to fix the situation? Find out what is wrong? Second-guess them and try to solve a problem that you have made up? You can quickly see how this might lead to a chain reaction that, at its least troublesome, would be a waste of energy, and at its most problematic would damage, or cause you to lose, the relationship with your client.

On the other hand, if you stop when you sense the closing sensation, feel your body, quiet your mind, and observe what you are thinking, you'll recognize that your IGS is letting you know that the thoughts you are having are not true, and that they are leading you away from success with your client. You can then begin focusing on finding the thoughts that open you, leading you to truer and more fulfilling, successful thoughts. In the beginning, simply reverse the thoughts you are having and see if this results in an opening sensation.

As you read further, it is important to remember that closing sensations (bad feelings in the area of your IGS: uneasiness, fear, anxiety, worry, stress, or concern) occur only when your thoughts are not true and are moving you away from success. If you are experiencing closing sensations in relation to someone or something, that means what you are thinking is not true, or that you need to reexamine it to find the perspective that reverses the sensation. If there is an actual problem, or when you are thinking about a problem, and your IGS gives you an opening sensation, then what you are thinking is true and is something you need to focus on solving. You can use your IGS to find out what the problem is. As you go through parts of the project or situation, you will open when you hit upon the thought that is true and needs to be addressed. It will open you. You will feel open and confident in the fact that there is action to be taken.

The Source of IGS Guidance

This is one of the most interesting aspects of your IGS. Where the guidance and wisdom come from is not something I can be completely sure of. What I do know from all my years of experience is that the guidance is wise, and that your IGS seems to know everything that must be taken into account in the situation so that everything will work out perfectly for everyone involved. These facts alone still astound me, even though I am used to the process by now. When you begin to follow your IGS, you quickly realize that it knows things about the past, present, and future that your mind could not possibly know. Your IGS understands more about you and your limiting beliefs or thoughts than you are able to understand about yourself.

I suggest that you explore your IGS and then decide for yourself where its guidance comes from. Speaking for myself, I can say that what creates the open sensation in me when I ponder this topic is the perception that my IGS is a broader, wiser, and infinite part of me: my higher Self, Divine Self, the Holy Spirit. The IGS or the way that it works is referenced in many wisdom traditions, from those of indigenous tribes to world religions. It is the energy that is running through all of life and is engaged in all aspects of our universe. It operates out of space and time, so it can see where your thoughts are leading you and the ramifications of continuing on a particular path. Guidance is given on every aspect of your life — not just the big things but the little things too.

I remember one instance where I got out of a business meeting early. On my way home, I thought I would stop by the grocery store and do my shopping so I would not have to leave the house again later. (I love missing the rush hour at the grocery store.) As I was thinking about which store to go to and what I would purchase, I realized my chest was tight and I was feeling stressed, the results of my IGS creating a closing sensation. I thought, "That's strange." Over the years I have learned not to try to figure out why I am feeling opened or closed, and that when I simply trust this guidance, things work out so much better. I thought, "Well, I guess I had better head home," and my chest area began to relax, which is the opening sensation of the IGS.

As I pulled onto my street, I saw the cable TV repairman in front of our home. The repairman was just picking up the orange cones and putting them in the back of his van. As I drove up to him, I rolled down my window and asked if he was there for our house. He said yes. He had gotten a report that our DVR was not working. This was a very big deal! My roommate was a basketball fan — a *big* basketball fan — and it was time for "March Madness." He was missing it while he was at work and clearly had made the appointment and forgot. I let the repairman in. He fixed the DVR and all was well with the world.

You cannot imagine how happy my roommate was that I had just *happened* to be there.

You will come to your own conclusions about where the IGS gets its information, or maybe you will decide to just let it be a mystery. Over time, coincidence, synchronicity, miracles, and just plain ol' luck will become common. You hit the post office, bank, grocery store — you name it — while there is no line. And five minutes later tons of people walk in and you are already on your way out. In fact, when you follow your IGS this will become so common that you will be shocked when something happens that is not that way — which generally means you have not been paying attention to your IGS, and it is time to get back on track.

Your IGS in Relation to Positive and Negative Thoughts

People often believe that the IGS is simply a matter of having positive or negative thoughts — that the opening and closing sensations are based on the quality of their thoughts. This is actually not the case. Your IGS can open when you are feeling emotionally upset, and it can close when you are feeling emotionally happy. The emotions you have are not the same as your IGS. Your emotions are separate and distinct from your IGS. Feeling hopeful has led many people into unhappy situations — and vice versa: feeling emotionally distraught has created wreckage in what otherwise were good situations.

Your IGS leads you regardless of how you are feeling. You can think positive thoughts in a situation that is not going to bring you fulfillment and success, and no matter how much you hope that it will, your IGS will not respond by creating an open sensation. As you learn to use your IGS over time, you will discover how this aspect works.

One student of mine learned this in a striking way. She recounts her experience:

Your IGS Always Moves You toward Fulfillment and Success

Your IGS is continually guiding you toward what is best for you and best for everyone around you. This may seem like too large a task for your own little IGS. However, let me assure you that it is the absolute truth.

What I have come to realize is that everyone in my life is there for a purpose. I am a part of others' lives for a purpose. If there is no purpose in the connection, they just seem to fade away, or we conflict in some way that keeps us from contacting one another, or we never really "stick" to begin with. You know what I mean — you meet someone you think is just great, but then you never contact them, or possibly never see them, after that. If you have a purpose in someone's life, then the two of you are together to grow, learn from one another, or support each other. An example of this is meeting someone who is going through what you went through in your past, and you are able to share your experience and have compassion for the challenges they are facing.

The guidance your IGS gives you is specific to your life. It takes into account how you are to think, feel, and behave in order to be happy and successful in every situation you encounter. If there is a difficult situation or conversation that you need to have, your IGS will lead you to the most satisfying and successful conclusion for you and everyone concerned. Now let me be clear: It may not seem that way when the moment is occurring. Yet if you let your IGS guide you in your thoughts and speech, you will find that this will absolutely be the outcome.

One of my clients was trying to make a very difficult decision. She had a job opportunity fifteen hundred miles from where she lived. The difficulty was that her husband, who loved his job, did not want to move, and their children were happy where they were living. Both children were thriving at school and had a community of friends who were important to them. Yet what opened her was the thought of taking the new position. Despite her opening, they could not believe that the move could possibly be good for all of them, but they decided to use their IGSs to look at it differently.

They went over and over the details together. Her husband got an opening sensation in response to the idea of her going, but he could not get over the idea of being left to raise their children alone most of the time. They both had lots of thoughts about how hard it would be and how they would be lonely, and they feared this could even end their marriage. All these consequences closed both of them, meaning that they were not true, and their thoughts of hardship were actually not moving them in the direction of success.

In the end they decided to pay attention to their sense of opening, and she took the position. They all got along fine, and their marriage actually blossomed! When making decisions about the children, they had to be very clear and aligned with one another; they planned beautiful, fun weekends when she came home (which they had rarely made time for in the past); and the two of them found ways to be better connected and more romantic together. Their new passion for each other was the result of realizing how much they truly meant to each other.

She stayed in the position for six months and then, out of nowhere, was offered another wonderful position in the area from which she had just come. Her taking that position opened both my client and her husband. They cite those six months apart as what brought their relationship back to life, united their family, and gave them a new way of prioritizing their relationship. The period they spent apart continues to be a gift in their lives to this day.

There may be times when you doubt the guidance you are getting from your IGS. You may feel apprehensive when you get a sense of opening that does not line up with what your mind thinks is safe or good. Over the years I have walked many people through these types of scenarios, and I can assure you they all turned out to be the best thing that could have happened, and that the people involved ended up being happier than before. You will soon find this out for yourself. So, on to part 2, where you will learn how to use your IGS.

PART TWO

USING YOUR IGS

When to Use Your IGS

The best time to use your IGS is *always*! If you use it only when you are confused, or don't know what to do, or are so closed that you feel horrible, you will miss the amazing benefits that can accrue when your life is full of synchronicities and miracles. The best way to incorporate your IGS into your life is as you are going about your day. Of course, it takes practice to remember to feel the sensations, but this quickly turns into a habit. The wonderful thing about your IGS is that you can feel it: it wakes you up when you are flowing toward something you don't desire.

Picture yourself going about your day. In the background you are worried about how well your child is doing in school. Perhaps you have been called to a parent-teacher conference, and your mind is running every scenario possible about what the teacher will discuss. Not only that, but your mind is also beating you up for every parenting "mistake" you believe you have made recently.

Suddenly, you realize you have a rock in your solar plexus, your chest is tight, and you are filled with anxiety. You have started practicing using your IGS and realize that you have a belief or body of thought that is *not true and not leading you toward fulfillment and success*! As you examine what you were thinking, you realize that all your thoughts were about getting in trouble for the way your child is acting in school, and that these thoughts have brought on emotions like shame, embarrassment, and failure. However, you realize that these beliefs are not true, because your solar plexus is closed. Your chest, too, is closed, so you realize that the meeting will not go the way it is being played out in your head. Rather than continue to worry, you decide to look for what causes you to open instead.

You focus on finding a new perspective, looking for what is really true:

- Everyone's kids have issues. My worries are similar to what all parents face at some point. This is a normal way to feel as a parent.
- Everyone feels like his or her parenting style can use some work.
- The teacher is there to help me, and we are on the same team.

As you hold these thoughts you begin to feel ease in your solar plexus and your chest, which of course lets you know that these thoughts are closer to reality than the previous thoughts. You are able to focus on work, you feel better, and you even feel the pleasant expectation that the meeting will go well.

This type of moment is the gold produced by using your IGS all the time. By not putting it on a shelf and taking it down only when you are in trouble or confused, you clean out the anxiety-ridden thoughts your mind produces. Pay attention to your body and to the sensations in the area of your IGS. That way you can keep your energy flowing and maintain your feeling of openness and creativity. Looking at the scenario above, can you imagine feeling more flexible, creative, and open when walking into the meeting with that new perspective? Be aware of your IGS throughout your day.

Deepening Your Listening Practice

Here is a meditation that will help you feel your IGS more easily. Read through the meditation in its entirety, and then go back and try it. If you are struggling and would like to listen to me walk you through it, go to the following website and listen to or download a free recording of this exercise: www.your innergps.org/listeningpractice.

First, make sure that anything around you that will distract you is put away or turned off. Sit in a comfortable chair, in a comfortable position with your feet on the floor. It's a good idea to choose a chair that has a back that's comfortable. Next, place your hands on your lap with your palms facing upward. Take a breath and just relax for a moment. When you're settled, feel the sensation of the bottom of your feet resting against the floor. Deeply experience the sensation of the pressure of your feet on the floor. Notice your toes, how they feel, and — whether they're in shoes or not — how your feet are resting against the floor; then notice the area where there is no pressure. For a few more moments bring your full awareness to the bottoms of your feet.

Next, bring your awareness to your hands, in particular your palms. Feel the sensation of the palms of your hands and notice if they feel more alive or filled with a light energy. Do this for a few moments.

Now feel your tailbone. Your tailbone is located at the base of your spine, and if you're sitting upright in your chair, it'll be right where the L part of your chair meets your body. Experience your tailbone at the base of your spine, feel and sense it at rest on the chair.

What I'd like you to do next is imagine that, attached to your tailbone, by a cord or a cable, is a big weighted object like a cannonball or a boat anchor. Feel the weight of it pulling you more deeply into your seat. Really experience it as if it's holding you still in your seat. When you're ready, release that anchor or that cannonball, keeping it attached to your tailbone, and allow it to fall and then settle into the earth, going farther and farther toward the center of the earth until it comes to its own natural resting place.

Next, we'll begin the listening portion of this meditation. I'd like you to experience the sounds around you both near and far, which means that you'll experience the sounds in the room you are in as well as listen to what's happening outside the room or the building or other place you're in. You may hear birds, the wind, cars, planes, or laughter. If you're in an apartment building, you may hear someone else's TV set or footsteps. If you listen closely to the room you are in, you may notice the sound of your refrigerator, the purring of your cat, the creaking of your home, or the hum of your computer.

I'd like you to listen to both the external and the internal, experiencing them at the same time. By *experiencing*, I mean:

don't name the things you're hearing; just allow your sense of hearing to experience them as if they were sound waves. This may seem complex, but very quickly your body will begin to pick up on things you are unaware of. If your mind begins to wander, focus on feeling your feet, the palms of your hands, and your tailbone. You'll find that by focusing on all three, and by listening both near and far, you'll feel a sense of peace or an experience of your mind quieting. Do this for two to ten minutes.

When you've completed this portion of the meditation, wiggle your toes, take a breath, open your eyes, and look around.

Now, what you may have found is that your mind wandered, whether you liked that or not. It may have started naming things. If that happens again, treat your mind as if it were a box of puppies — that's right, a box of puppies. If you were sitting there, watching these cute wiggling puppies, and one of them crawled out and scampered across the room, you wouldn't go and pick it up and say, "Bad puppy," spank it on the behind, and be frustrated with it. That's what puppies do — they explore. And that's what your mind does.

So if you're sitting there, practicing the listening exercise, have some patience with your mind. It may take a few sessions before your mind begins to quiet and relax. The key is to keep returning your focus to your feet, your hands, and your tailbone — all three — and then experiencing the sounds around you both near and far. Just continue to do that over and over. It is as simple as putting that puppy back in the box.

I know this may sound like a complex process. But one thing to keep in mind is that it actually becomes very quick and easy. I call the practices in this book "living practices" because you can do them anywhere. Once you have gotten good at the listening practice while sitting still, then begin practicing it on the go. You can practice while brushing your teeth: simply feel your hands, your feet, and your tailbone, and listen to what's around you. You can do it at work, while you're driving, sitting at the park, waiting in line at the grocery store — there are all kinds of places where you can drop into your listening. It doesn't have to take long to get into the meditation. It can be instant, as fast as you read, "Feet, hands, tailbone, drop anchor, listen." You can experience dropping into your listening meditation wherever you are. I've walked you through it slowly just so you'll understand the process. The goal is for you to instantly calm your mind while preparing a specific point to return to each time you stop to check with your IGS.

PRACTICE

Do this meditation at least once a day, while seated. When it feels easy, start doing it while in motion so you can drop into your listening anywhere, at any time, and quickly.

How to Start Using Your IGS Every Day

Remembering to become aware of your IGS throughout your day can be challenging, and it can take quite a bit of focus in the beginning. Your IGS has been with you since you were born, yet no one knew to teach you what the sensations meant. What happens for most people, since they do not know that the opening and closing actually mean something, is that they ignore the sensations. Or their minds begin assigning meaning to the openings and closings. For example, when they feel pressure in the chest, they believe that it means the person talking to them intends to hurt them or otherwise should not be trusted. Accurately interpreting the IGS's guidance requires learning to relate the sensations to what you are thinking, instead of to how the world around you is "making" you feel.

I have found that, in general, there are two ways people who are out of sync with their IGS deal with the unpleasant sensations of closing. One is by not feeling their bodies and instead living in their heads. The other is by living solely according to their emotions. In the first situation, people have trouble recognizing the sensations of the IGS at all. The result is that those people live completely in the realm of strategy, logic, and the imagination. People in the second situation may find themselves triggered by or overly emotional in response to the encounters they find themselves in.

The way to discover if you are one or the other (or possibly you switch back and forth between the two) is to look at how your daily life unfolds. If you find that your day zips by, and that you lose part of your day — meaning you just don't remember it — you may be part of the first group. You might be thinking, "What? How can you lose part of your day?" Have you ever driven home and then found you couldn't remember the drive home? Have you ever been flowing right along in a project and looked up to find that it was four o'clock in the afternoon, yet the last time you looked at the clock it was ten in the morning? This is classic behavior for those who spend their time living in their minds. There is nothing wrong with this at all — it is one way of living. However, learning to be aware of your body and your IGS will present you with distinct challenges.

To discern whether you are in the second situation, consider how much of your day is spent in an emotional state. Do you get upset by an event and lose your focus? Instead of continuing on with your day, do you find that your mind keeps interrupting your focus by rerunning the offensive encounter, mentally arguing with the other person, listing all the reasons why the person is wrong or has no right to treat you that way, or projecting how things are going to end, with some sort of painful resolution?

I am someone who has both types of mental experiences. Even after fifteen years of training others to use their IGS, I have moments when I overlook the fact that the thoughts I am having are creating a closing sensation, and I can become overly emotional. I do realize it rather quickly, but if the triggering thoughts are in one of my weak areas, I can forget for a period of time. It is not a bad thing to be either type of person or even both. I am outlining the types only because knowing what your pattern is can help. Once you recognize it, you can move past it. If you are the first type, then it's important to begin by bringing your awareness to your body throughout the day. The "Deepening Your Listening Practice" meditation on page 64 is a wonderful way to begin. If you are able to take time to do the active meditation throughout the day, it will greatly help you feel your body. You can do it anywhere, without anyone knowing you're doing it. You can listen to it or download it for free at www.yourinnergps.org/listeningpractice.

As you remember to focus on your body, you will find that each time you check in you'll feel an IGS sensation. Remember, there are openings, closings, and neutrals. Even if you just feel neutral, you are feeling your IGS. Once you are feeling your IGS sensations more often, move on to the next practice, described below.

If you are a person whose mind has attached emotions to the sensations of your IGS, it is still important to quiet yourself and feel your body. Often, we feel a great deal during emotional experiences, and what we feel is our emotional energy; we are not grounded in our bodies. So start by feeling your feet, being aware of your breath, and listening to the sounds in the area around you. Next, notice the sensation of your IGS. Don't assume that it will be closed. Your mind may be raging with the thoughts that have caused the emotions, so try to stay with your body and witness how you are feeling and your IGS's guidance regarding your thoughts. I have often been surprised when experiencing the emotions of hurt, anger, or frustration, only to realize I was open and that these feelings were authentic. By experiencing them in combination with an opening sensation from my IGS, I was able to know they were true and own them fully. I could then release them in a good way, and, in so doing, avoid the "negative emotions" that would damage my health, relationships, and ultimately my happiness.

If you have many emotional upsets, start with the listening practice and be aware of your IGS, discovering the guidance under the emotional energy. Are you open, or are you closed by the thoughts you are having? If you are open, stay with the emotion but be aware of your thoughts. They can quickly shift and cause you to close. You'll want to catch what is true, and what is not, in the situation. Very often, if you simply realize that your thoughts are true and in alignment, a calmness of being, if not a calming of your emotions, begins to occur.

Stating When You Are Closed

This particular exercise is called "Noticing Closing Sensations as Guidance." It's amazing, actually, that one of the most difficult things for people to learn and become accustomed to is that the feelings of anxiety, worry, and fear, as well as the symptoms of stress, all are sensations of closing caused by the Internal Guidance System. What would it be like if, for the rest of your life, whenever you feel stress, worry, anxiety, or fear, you could release those unpleasant sensations almost instantly and feel calm and happy instead?

Let's look at this within a real-life situation and see what happens inside when you realize you're going to arrive late somewhere. Think of a situation where it is important for you to arrive on time, such as work or an event where people are counting on you. Play this scenario in your mind as if it is happening. Notice how your body begins to feel — the anxiousness that can even feel like dread. "Oh no, I'm going to disappoint people. I need to get there on time. How am I going to make this work?" Notice the closing sensations prompted by your Internal Guidance System. This means that your thoughts about the situation — what you're thinking about how this will affect others, what is going to happen as a result of your being late, and what steps you need to take to fix it — are not true. Not only are they not true, but they are also leading you away from what is going to work in the situation. This is one of the times when you may not realize you are closed. You have been reacting to being late in a particular way for a lifetime.

Since our minds are habitual systems that reproduce the same thoughts, reactions, and even emotions in the same way, most of the time it is challenging to think, "I am closing — this means my thought is not true." Your mind will lead you somewhere before you're even aware that you're being led. The "Noticing Closing Sensations as Guidance" practice will make it so much easier to recognize when you are being led down a closing path, so it's an especially important exercise. I recommend that you do it for one solid week. Begin by simply identifying when you're closed. As you go about your life and you notice that you're feeling closed, at that moment take a second and state to yourself: "I am closed; this means that what I am thinking is not true and is not bringing me toward success and happiness."

When you feel that tightening in your chest, become conscious of the fact that the sensations are connected to guidance. The more comfortable you become with naming the sensations of anxiety, stress, worry, or fear as the closing of your IGS, the quicker you'll stop your mind from taking over and dominating your life with old habitual thoughts. By identifying those sensations, you will be able to correct the thoughts that are not true and then find thoughts that will open you, in this way determining what is actually truer in the moment.

When you make the statement "I am closed; this means that what I am thinking is not true and is not bringing me toward success and happiness," you will almost immediately feel an easing sensation, an opening in the area where you felt the closing. The reason you open is because that simple statement is true, and it is a switch that, whenever it is used, will help you realize that your IGS is giving you guidance. When you become conscious of the guidance, the first step of the journey begins.

Those sensations have been happening for your entire life. As a result, your mind already has a response to them, and it is going to tell you they mean something different from what your IGS will tell you.

Your mind has learned to protect you by using survival tactics when it feels worry, stress, fear, and anxiety. This is because it was never told that these sensations are guidance instead of danger. It *is* important that you realize those sensations actually mean you need to stop and begin thinking about the entire situation in a new way. Please don't try to find openings at first. You will open slightly, as previously mentioned, because the "I am closed" statement that you will utter is true. But for now, just practice finding thoughts that make you close. Make a game of it. How many can you find in a day?

PRACTICE

Whenever you're feeling the closing sensation of anxiety, stress, fear, or worry, say, "I'm closed; this means that what I'm thinking is not true and is not bringing me toward success

and happiness." If you have to say that sentence over and over
— like an affirmation or a mantra — before you begin to feel
the opening sensation and the tightness eases, please do that. A
part of this exercise is actually you sensing the way your IGS
responds when you give it a new thought.

What Was I Thinking?

The next step in developing your awareness of your IGS is to become conscious of what you are thinking. In the last practice, you might have experienced a closing but been unable to recall the thought that corresponded to it. Since your IGS is giving you guidance on your thoughts, it's important to realize what your thoughts are. This may seem like a simple endeavor, but surprisingly it's challenging. Most people find that they are cruising along in life when suddenly they realize that they are closed. And when they try to find the thoughts that triggered the closing, they cannot remember them. When this happens, don't think you are crazy or alone. It still happens even to me on occasion. We are not used to paying close attention to what our minds are really doing as we live our lives.

At first, the most important element is the realization that you are closed. Why, you might ask, is it not equally important to notice when we're open? When we feel good, we have a tendency to just keep moving right along. It is when we feel unpleasant that we wake up and pay attention. A closing is our alarm bell — our wake-up call — and an alarm often makes it easier to pay attention to the guidance our IGS is giving. The openings, too, will become more and more important as you gain conscious access to your IGS.

If you find at first that you cannot remember what you were thinking, there are several reasons for this. Different levels and types of thoughts are happening all at once. Some of these you actually are aware of, such as what you are going to have for lunch, the next task on your to-do list, or what you need to say to someone the next time you speak to her. Then there are thoughts under the surface that you don't pay attention to.

When thinking about lunch, you may be thinking about your diet versus what you are craving to eat. Then there are the tasks you need to accomplish and, subsequently, the challenges you know you'll face while completing those tasks. Or you may desire a specific outcome and simultaneously fear it won't happen. When talking with someone, you listen and freely respond. However, in the background of your mind you may be worrying about what they will think of your answers, or perhaps past experiences are coming to mind that influence how you are responding.

Another issue that arises is that when we think, we also feel, we remember, we make connections, we develop opinions, and we pull from the past and project into the future. The IGS is responding to all of this, and the thought that it responds to at any given moment may not be on the surface or otherwise easily accessible at first. Most of us are unaware of how our minds actually work and don't pay particular attention to what we are thinking.

Additionally, we simply are not conscious of our minds on a regular basis. Most of us just live and let our minds do whatever they want. It is not like we are encouraged to pay attention to this powerful part of who we are. In the past, we didn't know that we needed to, and so we didn't; in this way we set up the persisting pattern of not paying attention to our minds and how they operate. Therapy can be powerful in this regard, because it gives us a chance to reflect on what we are thinking and to question whether we would like to think differently. Most of us were not taught as children to listen to ourselves or to reflect on who we are inside.

When you begin to slow down, feel your body, and experience your IGS, a natural progression is to next examine the thoughts that open or close you. It is a powerful path of self-discovery. The key is to not judge what you are thinking — do not worry about the content of the thoughts that close you. Just recognize that your IGS is telling you that the thought is not true and is not leading you toward a happy outcome. At this point, you have a choice. When you find the thought that closed you, you can play with different perspectives or ways of thinking about the situation or person or that person's motives. When one of these perspectives brings a sense of relief or opening, build on that thought. Use the momentum of the opening to change how you are thinking about things.

When you have a closing sensation and cannot remember what you were thinking, simply take note. What I have found is that most people's minds play on a loop. The thought you lost will come back. We have very few new or creative thoughts unless we go out of our way to have them. This aspect of your mind will change as you begin to use your IGS more. Until then, be patient, notice that a thought is missing, notice the situation you are in, and then wait. Generally, in less than a day the thought will be back and you can take note of it then.

PRACTICE

Begin to notice what you are thinking, and if you cannot find the thought, stop and notice the situation you are in and what you are doing. You will close again when the thought repeats — and it will — and you will catch it then. Over time, you will develop a deeper awareness of what your mind produces, and this practice will become unnecessary.

Discovering Your Closing Themes

Most people have themes in life that are stressful, such as finances, family, relationships, career, children, health, and overall future well-being, to name just a few. Even more interesting is that within these themes are subthemes that make up who we are inside. Stress is interesting, and difficult to define medically, because it is unique to each person. We each have a different set of stress factors, and our bodies' reactions to stress differ as well. The next practice is about you getting to know your own stressors, your intimate, personal themes that cause you to close.

Over the next few days take time to record the things that are stressing you out. If you notice that your thoughts revolve around your body image, and this is stressful to you, then make a note of it. Putting it in writing can help you link your thoughts together. Are your thoughts about your children, their health and well-being? Is money the main theme that runs through your mind, causing your closing thoughts? What is it that brings on your closings? You will discover the three or four main themes that create the sensation of stress, which is really

your IGS closing. Knowing your themes will make it much easier to recognize your closings as they are happening.

In the course of my work I have found that most people
have blind spots where, without help, they can't see that they
are closed. They do know that they are not happy. They are
suffering, feeling unwell, depressed, anxious, or afraid. Or they
may know that they're closed, but they can't naturally make
the leap to recognizing that it is their thoughts that are creating
the unpleasant and unhappy way they feel. They truly believe
the misinformation their minds are giving them and forget to
even question the thoughts. So they will book a session with me
to help them figure out what they are thinking and what is happening. The first thing I do is let them know that the thoughts
currently troubling them are not true. This comes as a genuine
surprise to them. Often that's all they need to know in order to
begin experiencing openings again. Once they begin to think,
"I'm closed; all the thoughts I'm having are not true," they realize that they can think something else at that moment or let it
go altogether.

It becomes much easier for you to recognize when you're
closed once you know your themes and blind spots. If you
know that your money situation and children are the two main
themes that close you, then when those themes arise in your
thinking, and you're feeling closed, you can immediately recognize it. This helps you start a new habit, one that shifts the
way your mind thinks. Most of us are so used to just rolling
along with our stress, worry, fear, or anxiety, and not questioning those feelings, that we need help to remember.

You may think you have one theme but, on closer exam-
ination, realize it is actually something else. You may find you

have many stressful conversations and then notice they are stressful because you fear that "everyone" is angry, or going to be angry, with you. So your theme is "the fear that others are angry with me," not "stress over conversing with others." In this example, if your IGS is causing you to close when you think others are angry with you, that means they are not actually angry with you. Even though they are not, at first you may have difficulty believing it, since this has been a theme for years. You may feel as if you must be correct in your thinking — you may dive into your closing thoughts, ruminating on the theme, not realizing that the thoughts are closing you and are not true. I call this being hijacked by your mind. It can take time to wake up from these thoughts when they happen.

For years I thought people who did not call me back right away were upset with me. The thought always closed me, but my mind would incessantly bug me with these thoughts. Finally I realized what was happening and stopped these thoughts by using my IGS. I was so much happier once these thoughts had been eliminated from my mind. You can begin to reinvent your thoughts by reversing them as I just did: "angry/closed" means "not angry/open." I think to myself: "That thought is closing me, so this means they are actually not angry, no matter how frequently my mind tells me they are. I can let the thought go, because it is closing."

The cool thing about your IGS and your mind is that, before long, they become friends of a sort. Your mind begins to look to your IGS for support. When that happens, you notice that the closing sensations no longer feel so unpleasant and they don't mean as much as they used to. Things calm down as the two work together to find new perspectives. We will work on more practices that open you, shortly.

PRACTICE

Spend the next few days to a week recognizing and writing down what you're thinking when you are feeling stress, worry, fear, and anxiety. As you write, put things into categories — you'll notice certain themes emerging. Sometimes it takes writing down the thoughts, experiences, and situations before the themes will emerge.

Four Terms That Often Cause Closing

There are four terms you can look for in your thinking and speaking that can uncover your mental equivalents of the obsolete yellow yield signs: *should, have to, need to,* and *must.* These words often cause our IGS to close us. Why is this? As children we are taught about life from other people's perspectives. We are taught what is a good thing and what is a bad thing, what it takes to be happy, what will bring us love, and what will bring us success. In the midst of learning all these things, we also learn what we should, have to, need to, and must do to thrive, be loved, and be happy. The problem is we never question whether other people's values or ideas are right for us.

If you use one of these words and notice that your IGS causes you to close, then it is time to examine whether what you are thinking about is actually true for you.

One of the gifts of using your Internal Guidance System is that it will bring you back to your true, authentic Self. It guides you to become who you are at your core. And since our minds are already made up about what's right for us, it can be difficult, without the IGS, to get to the truth of who we are. Your

IGS will lead you to question parts of your thinking that you may never have dreamed of questioning. These unquestioned beliefs are the equivalents of the outdated yellow yield sign I mentioned earlier. (Many people thought it was yellow and black and not white and red.) When the four terms *should*, *have to*, *need to*, and *must* cause you to close, you are being led to question things about your life that exist in your blind spots.

For instance, let's say you think, "I have to rewrite my résumé and find a new job." Notice whether you're open or closed. If you are open, then move into action toward what opens you. If you're closed, it's time to look at which part of the sentence is closing you and to find the thought that opens you. Use it to replace the untrue thought. It could be as simple as doing the opposite. Say to yourself, "I don't need to find a new job." Open. Okay. Then examine why you are looking to find a new job. In following your thinking toward the openings, you will find your most successful path to satisfaction. If that does not work, be creative. Maybe you don't need a new résumé. Or maybe the new job you are considering — the thought of which causes you to open — is an internal transfer within the company where you already work. No résumé needed.

Anytime over the next week that you hear yourself saying any of those four terms, stop, drop into your listening, and notice — open or closed? In doing this, you may find that your beliefs about what you should be doing, have to do, need to do, or must do are actually not true. They are preconceived ideas and beliefs that were given to you by others. Let them go, and find the truth. Examine your assumptions. Reconfigure your thinking around the subject.

Sometimes it requires getting creative to find what is true

for you at the moment. Make sure that you're aware of when you use those four terms in relation to other people ("he should be..."), outside situations ("they need to..."), and the world around you ("we must..."). When you use them in your thinking, and you speak about the world around you, you may find that many of your most triggering beliefs begin with closing guidance — meaning what or how you are thinking is incorrect and out of alignment. Once you find the thoughts that open you, they will align you with what is going to create success and happiness for you and the people in the world around you.

PRACTICE

Notice anytime you think or say the four terms *should*, *have to*, *need to*, or *must*. Notice if you're closed or open. If open, that's wonderful! You're right on track. If you are closed, then stop and reverse the thought to the opposite of what you were thinking. If that does not provide ease, then play creatively with your belief about what you "should," "have to," "need to," or "must" do, until you feel yourself open up again.

HELPFUL HINT

When doing this practice, ask a friend or another person you trust to gently point out when you're using one of those four terms. Or you can write them on cards and put them up in a few areas — such as your car, office, fridge, and nightstand — so that you can remember to notice them. Most of the practices I ask you to do involve working with your mind, and your mind has already determined what it believes. To examine your mind, you have to use tricks to remember to do the practices. But try not to judge yourself when you hear yourself saying any of the four terms. In fact, if you do judge, you'll probably notice that your judgment starts off with I *should*, *have to*, *need to*, or *must*. So examine those thoughts as well. Enjoy the practice.

Emotions and Your IGS

Your emotions are not the same as your Internal Guidance System, and distinguishing between the two is very important. Many people believe, in the beginning, that they feel an opening or a closing based on what they feel emotionally in a situation. This assumption is not necessarily inaccurate at the start. Since most of us have linked the guidance provided by the IGS with emotions, you may find that in the beginning they often match. Rather quickly in your journey, though, you will find they are not the same.

Your emotions are actually caused by a biochemical reaction that takes place in the brain and then floods the body. Experiencing these biochemical reactions is a lot like taking a drug such as alcohol. Think about times when you have been in the throes of an emotion and were unable to shift that emotion. Even when the cause of the emotional experience is removed, the residue of the energy is still present for quite some time. This is not the way your IGS behaves. Your IGS shifts without any residue. Yes, some may feel as if they are still closed after the cause is removed. However, if you really check in with yourself, you'll recognize that you're experiencing residue from the chemical that the brain released, in the form of an emotion.

What is most important at first is for you to realize that when you are feeling emotional, it will take time for the emotion-inducing chemicals that were released to dissipate. As you explore your IGS, you will become aware of your emotions and discover that, quite simply, emotions are just additional pieces of information for you to check against your IGS. I have a perfect example of how this unfolded in my own life.

When I was young, I thought I was a jealous person. The reactions I had in response to my boyfriends' behavior sure seemed like jealousy. Well, I am not a person who sits by and lets some aspect of myself give others or me pain. I at least try to make peace with it. So off I went to read books about the subject and attend workshops, trying on different perspectives and practices in order to shift the jealousy I felt. Of course, all my boyfriends called my thoughts, feelings, and actions jealousy. I had told them I was jealous. Why would they not believe me?

One day after years of failing to resolve my jealousy, I was reading an article about insecurity. All the symptoms I had attributed to jealousy were those of insecurity. Then it hit me: I was insecure! What amazed me most about this realization was that when I had the thought that I was insecure, my IGS opened me with a rush of energy; I felt a giant expansion. I got so excited that I immediately called my current boyfriend and excitedly told him how insecure I was. He promptly replied, "Uh, is this a trick? 'Cause, well, didn't you know that?"

My point is that finding out I was not jealous, and that I was insecure instead, made all the difference. The way you deal with jealousy is very different from dealing with insecurity. Jealousy is about possessing or controlling someone, while insecurity is about self-worth. I had spent years trying to solve something that was not really my problem. Emotionally, it had seemed like the same thing. I realized that my IGS had closed me whenever I thought about being jealous. But it never dawned on me that my thoughts about being jealous were not true, or that the horrible, anxiety-ridden feelings I was having about that jealousy were the effects of my IGS's attempts to guide me. Needless to say, I embarked on a path to become more secure and to understand my self-worth. As a result, I no longer endure the same emotional pain.

What is my point? On my path to resolving my insecurity, I frequently felt both the insecurity and the opening sensation as I thought to myself, "This is my insecurity; this is not something my boyfriend is doing to me or doing wrong." Even while I was in the throes of the inner tantrums that resulted from insecurity, the openings pointed me to new thoughts, healing that part of me.

As mentioned earlier, you can have pleasant or unpleasant emotions, but your IGS remains independent of the emotion-inducing chemicals that flood your body in response. As you learn to trust your IGS, you can ask yourself questions about the emotions you have. Start by figuring out what you are feeling. Then, when you have named what you are feeling — frustration, despair, abandonment, or even hope, happiness, or peace — check in with your IGS to ensure that what you are experiencing is true and is leading you toward fulfillment and success.

One last note on this: You may not understand how you could feel happiness and peace and yet not have the sensation of opening. Have you ever really wanted to be in a relationship with someone and been really happy when he or she called, yet had this tight, uncomfortable feeling no matter how well things were going? Or have you had that feeling even when you were with him or her? Yep, that's what I am talking about. That person was not the right one at the time, and your IGS was letting you know that your thoughts and feelings about him or her were not going to lead you toward fulfillment or success.

Your Emotions Are a Gateway

One of the ways I discovered to bypass the craziness of the mind — all the doubt and worry and fear that come up in response to the guidance you get from your IGS — is to go through the door of your emotions. I use emotions as a gateway to help people clear out their obsolete yellow yield signs. As I noted earlier, when we feel an emotion, we are experiencing a biochemical reaction produced by the mind, and the emotion may or may not be true. This biochemical reaction is very often based on historical evidence that your mind has created — that you have a reason to be fearful, that you have a reason to be angry, that you're in love, that you're happy, or that you're disappointed. There are all kinds of ways in which our minds induce this biochemical feedback or emotion in our bodies, and they are based on stories from our past — on what we believe we've seen, heard, and felt, especially concerning the behavior of the people who raised us.

Very often our emotions are actually not in alignment and so do not open us. Instead, they were first triggered when we were younger and misinterpreted those thoughts that closed us.

Your mind hijacks the sensation of closing (worry, fear, anxiety, and stress) and combines it with its own fabricated evidence to make you believe that it knows what the future holds. It projects as fact what it thinks is going to happen. But in reality, it's running a habitual program that is repeated over and over in similar situations. If you have done the "Discovering Your Closing Themes" practice on page 80, then you already know that repeating thoughts are currently operating in your life.

The practice I'd like you to try now is to write out your feelings. Any time you're having an emotional experience — whether it feels positive or negative according to your mind — write what you're feeling. Use the list of emotions provided on page 97 to help you isolate more precisely what you are feeling. Most people are unaware of how they feel, or they have a limited emotional vocabulary. In order to boost your emotional vocabulary, use the list. I recommend that you copy it from this book, or you can go to www.yourinnergps.org /emotionslist and download the list so that you can post it in several places for reference. The office, fridge, bathroom, and nightstand are good; your car, purse, and wallet are some other great places to access it quickly. When you're in the midst of, or just over, an emotional experience, sit down with a piece of paper, look at the list, and write out the top three things you're feeling, such as "I'm feeling frustrated, I'm feeling disappointed, I'm feeling hurt."

Then write out why you're feeling those three emotions. Just let your mind tell you the story of why you feel the way you do. You don't have to make it a long story. In fact, it is best if it's just one or two sentences long.

"I'm feeling disappointed because this project was canceled, and it was very important to me. I'm feeling frustrated because it seems to me as if my manager is pulling out the projects that I really enjoy, and he seems to be doing it on purpose. I'm feeling hurt because I work very hard in this world and yet I don't seem to get the recognition or the rewards that I deserve."

The next step — and this is where your IGS comes into play — is to drop into your listening and read back to yourself each of the emotions/stories that you have written. Notice whether you are open or closed with each emotion and story.

What I have observed is that very often a negative emotional experience gets combined with a sense of closing caused by your IGS. This means what you're thinking is not true. The thoughts that prompted the closing, if continued, will not bring you to a happy resolution. If you don't get to the bottom of your thoughts and understand what is closing you, then your mind can actually drive you into a situation you don't want. Keep this in mind: when you get upset, you can use your emotions as a signal that it's time to stop and check your IGS.

One thing you'll discover in doing this exercise is that some of those statements will open you. I'll use the previous example to demonstrate how this may happen. You may get an opening sensation when you say you are disappointed; even though you feel disappointed, you will feel open. Then, when you tell your story about feeling frustrated, you will be closed. What closes you is the claim that the manager is specifically taking projects away from you. The closing means your manager is not undermining you on purpose, so you can drop that line of thinking and move on.

The feeling of disappointment, then, is authentic for you, and you can own it: "I have a right to be disappointed. The sensation of opening I feel when I make this statement tells me that disappointment is an authentic emotion in this case."

Do this exercise with positive emotions as well. You may be shocked at how many times you're really excited about something while guidance from your IGS is actually telling you that it is not going to happen or is not true.

So it's equally important to say, "I feel hopeful, I feel excited, and I feel joyous." Then write, "Okay, why am I feeling hopeful?" and answer this question. For example: "I'm feeling hopeful because, for the first time, I'm being recognized by the particular person I've been wanting to notice me for a very long time." Ask and answer the same question about feeling excited: "Why am I excited? I'm feeling excited because this person is noticing me, so maybe they want to date me. I'm totally attracted to them and know this is going to happen." Then look at feeling joyous: "I feel joyous because they could possibly be my soul mate."

Now once again drop into your listening and check your emotions and stories via your IGS. You may feel an opening at the thought that this person has been noticing you, but you may close when you think this means you will begin dating. Go through each statement, one at a time. "This person is noticing me." Open. Then look at the next part of the statement: "Maybe they want to date me." Closed. Oh, that's not why they're paying attention to me. "They could possibly be my soul mate." Closed. You feel tightening, or anxiety, in your chest.

Maybe the scenario above seems far-fetched to you, or maybe it sounds exactly like what your mind does to you. Either way, we all have situations where our minds make up instant stories and then, immediately after that, invent ramifications for our future, whether positive or negative. This type of thought process happens so quickly that we often miss it. Then we begin living the story as if it were real, and our lives can go off track for a bit. One purpose of your IGS is to clear out all the fictitious stories that your brain generates. This allows you to be very clear and effective in your life. One way to find the stories that close you is to do the following practice to address your emotions.

PRACTICE

Whenever you have an emotional experience that you would label as positive or negative, stop and write down the top three emotions that you're feeling (use the emotions list on the next page). Then, for each emotion, uncover the story of why you feel as you do, and write it down. If possible, keep it short — one or two sentences — being as forthright about that statement as you can.

Once you've written those three stories down, drop into your listening and use your IGS to find out whether they open or close you. Record the first sensation you feel. If you sit with it too long, you are guessing. Drop into your listening and look at the emotion and story again. It is important to go with the first sensation you have.

Notice whether you feel a sense of ease or a sense of constriction. This will give you greater clarity about the situation and enable you to take authentic and effective action. Do this for two weeks. It's one of the most crucial awakenings you'll experience when using your IGS, so take your time. Please don't move on to the next exercise until you have some experience with how this one works for you.

HELPFUL HINT

Do not try to be politically correct, and do not edit the story that comes up or try to be nice about how you are feeling. Be as honest as possible about how you feel, and resist editing it down to less than it is. If your mind is using cuss words or inappropriate solutions, or thinking downright ugly thoughts, use them in this exercise. It's okay. It is just your mind, not you. Relax and be real about what is going on in there. You don't need to show it to anyone, but you do need to get to the bottom of what you're feeling. Trust that your IGS will shift and erase what you don't like about yourself in the situation. State the story as accurately as possible according to what your mind is actually saying is going on. By being real, you will have bigger openings and closings, a better sense of release, and more clarity, and as a result you'll get healthier.

List of Emotions

absorbed	altruistic	balanced
abusive	analytical	beautiful
accepting	angry	belligerent
accommodating	annoyed	bereft
accomplished	antagonistic	bitter
adaptable	anxious	bored
adversarial	approved of	brave
aggressive	arrogant	broken down
agreeable	ashamed	bullied
alert	authentic	calm

chaotic
cheerful
cold
commanding
compassionate
competitive
complaining
conceited
condemned
condemning
confident
conflicted
confused
conservative
content
controlled
controlling
cooperative
courageous
cowardly
creative
critical
cruel
curious
defeated
deluded
demanding
dependent
depressed
desperate
destitute

destructive
detached
dignified
disconnected
discouraged
disgusted
dominated
dominating
eccentric
ecstatic
egocentric
egotistical
empathic
empowered
enraged
envious
erratic
excited
expressive
extroverted
fair
faithful
fearful
frightened
frustrated
glad
good
grateful
greedy
grieving
guilty

happy
harmonious
hateful
helpful
helpless
hesitant
hopeless
idealistic
ignorant
impatient
important
impoverished
impulsive
indifferent
individualistic
inert
insecure
insensitive
inspired
interested
intolerant
introspective
invulnerable
irresponsible
irritated
isolated
jealous
joyful
judged
judgmental
lazy

likable

lively

lonely

lost

loved

loving

mad

manipulated

manipulative

meditative

miserable

mistrusting

moody

moral

negative

noble

obsessed

open

panicked

paranoid

passionate

passive

peaceful

perfectionistic

pitiful

pleased

poor

possessive

powerful

practical

preoccupied

proud

punished

punishing

purposeful

reactionary

reclusive

rejected

rejoicing

repressed

resentful

resigned

resistant

responsible

ridiculous

righteous

ruthless

sabotaging

sad

sadistic

secretive

self-accepting

self-condemning

self-confident

self-defeating

self-destructive

self-hating

selfish

self-obsessed

self-pitying

sensitive

serene

shamed

shut down

shy

sorry

stable

stimulated

stricken

strung-out

stubborn

superior

temperamental

timid

tolerant

unconcerned

understanding

unforgiving

unhappy

unresponsive

untrusting

vain

vengeful

vicious

victimized

violent

visionary

well-meaning

wise

withdrawn

worthy

Using Your IGS for Time Management

You may wonder why I am going from emotions to time management. I find that time management is one of the most emotional aspects of my life and of the lives of many others. Whether we are always on time or never on time, we all have stress and differing levels of anxiety in response to time management. What I have learned is that time management can be boiled down to all of the "shoulds," "have tos," "need tos," and "musts" of our lives. Very rarely are any of us capable of trading these in for the "want tos," "love tos," and the ever-exciting "cannot wait tos." Yes, of course we all go on vacations or have that rare afternoon when there is nothing else that is pressing, and we let ourselves indulge in these. But what about how we spend the rest of our time?

Better management of time is one of the best things you can use your IGS for. It has changed my life and the lives of thousands of people! Your IGS, thank the heavens, is ever ready to help you enjoy and prioritize your to-do list and have a healthy and happy experience in life.

If your mind is anything like mine or the minds of my

clients, then you know that on any given day it will give you a multitude of "shoulds," "have tos," "need tos," and "musts." You may have heard the phrase "stop shoulding on yourself." Well, this is where that phrase takes on new meaning. As you move through your day, your mind is running nonstop, listing your never-ending to-do items. As the thoughts race through your mind, notice your IGS and its guidance on what is a priority and what is not. You will find that many of the items on your running list are closing you. Now, what exactly does that mean?

As I explained earlier, where your IGS gets its guidance from sits outside of space and time. It is calculating what needs to happen and when it needs to happen. Think of it as your time-management traffic cop. It signals you regarding what is to happen next and then next and then next. You'll find that when you let it do its magic, everything that needs to be done magically gets accomplished, and what does not need to be accomplished right then magically drops off your list.

This is how it works. As you go about your day, and your mind begins running through its list, you stop, feel your feet, breathe, and listen to the room around you. Then, as you begin again to run through your list, again feel the guidance from your IGS. If you feel yourself close in response to the idea of doing something specific on your list, move to the next item until your IGS gives you an opening. This may sound tedious at first, but it soon becomes second nature and you will naturally create your day this way.

You may be thinking, "Sure, I can do this in my personal life. But in business, it is just not possible with all the demands on me, given the reality of timelines and accountability to others." Or you may be thinking, "Yeah, right. I'm a parent. My time is not my own. I have practices, recitals, homework, cooking, cleaning, and making sure there is structure in my kids' life." No matter what the demands on your life are, I can tell you that it works. I ran a multimillion-dollar business and got everything done. Recently I had a baby, finished this book, managed the purchase of ten acres and the building of a house, then moved and restarted a six-figure business, all on an eighteen-month timeline. I used my IGS to make decisions and discover what needed my attention when. It may sound like it had to have been a challenging, miserable time, or that I could not have done it all. But the truth is, it was the most productive, happy year of my life and my family's. The only time there was pain was when I let my mind try to dictate my to-do list and project a dire future if things were left undone — rather than using my IGS.

When I was a consultant, I once had a project with a tight, fourteen-day timeline. Every day I woke up and checked with my IGS to determine what to do that day, and I closed every time I thought about getting started on this project. This happened every day for ten days. Needless to say, I started stressing, which was the result of my IGS's guidance on the project. Each time my mind began running rampant about the consequences of not starting on the monumental amount of work the project would require, especially given the short timeline, I realized I was closed. What the closing meant is that my thoughts were not true or leading me to success. This type of situation is confusing if you attempt to use logic.

I am a woman who walks her talk. Believe me, in the beginning it was challenging. On day ten, still with no opening sensation guiding me to begin the project, I got a phone call. Let me tell you, I was not excited when I saw the company's number come up on caller ID. The person on the phone asked how much I had accomplished on the project. I said honestly, "I have not done anything. Every day I just felt like I was not supposed to be working on it yet." To my surprise I heard relief in the person's voice. She said, "Thank goodness! We have just had a corporate meeting, and we are going to scrap the entire project."

Much to my relief, my IGS had stopped me from working on something that was not going to be fruitful. Yes, I would have been paid for my time, but what company wants to work with someone they've paid for producing something they could not use? In the end they asked me to use the retainer to do another project, and everyone was happy. I woke up the next day and felt myself opening at the prospect of starting work on the new project. That is the IGS at work.

I have story after story just like this one from my own life, and I have heard such stories from hundreds of others. Using your IGS works in all aspects of your life. Calling on it to help with your time management starts when you realize that anytime you are feeling stressed, rushed, or worried, you are closed. Yes, your IGS is giving you closing sensations. Stop and look at what you are thinking about cramming in — picking up the dry cleaning, making dinner, going to an appointment, and so on — while cutting out time for yourself so you can do these other things instead. There are endless ways that you can use your IGS to discover if the way you're thinking about your time is opening or closing you.

When you feel that rushed sensation, realize that your IGS

is asking you to find a new perspective. For example, "I am not supposed to do that chore now." Or: "I will make it on time," or "Dinner will happen," or "My part of the project will be ready just as it is needed." Feel whether the new perspective creates an opening in your IGS. If it does, trust it! Move on to being present to your day, and allow the guidance you are receiving to support you in focusing on what counts.

PRACTICE

Take a piece of paper and write out your to-do list. List as many "shoulds," "have tos," "need tos," and "musts" that you can conjure up. Then go through each one, drop into your listening, and see if it needs to be done at all. Are you open, closed, or neutral in response to it? Next to the task, put the letter *O* for "open," *C* for "closed," or *N* for "neutral." Do the tasks that open you, let go of the ones that close you, and ask more questions about the ones that leave you feeling neutral. For instance, "I need to clean the garage." Neutral. Okay: "My kids and husband need to clean the garage." Open. Play with different ideas to prompt your IGS to open or close you. Start each day by listing on paper what you think you need to do. Soon you will be doing this while in action in your life.

Voices in Your Head

One of the key ways I use my IGS is to stop the various voices in my head. Now, I don't know about your mind, but my mind tends to be a little schizophrenic. For example, when I'm lying in bed in the morning, half of me wants to jump out because I have all these things I want to do, but the other half wants to stay in bed and get more sleep. I used to find myself in the middle of mental arguments like this, going back and forth.

In talking with many other people, I've found that most have this same experience with all kinds of things in life: eating healthy foods or not, exercising or not, deciding how much to work and how much to play — our choices range between staying away from things that are bad for us and doing more of what is good for us. Using your IGS, you may find there are days when you need to get out of bed and days when you can sleep in. Your IGS knows the right decision and can help you tell the difference.

I'd like to share with you two voices that I have in my head — the child and the critic. I am sure there are more, but these two are fairly dominant for most people. As you inspect your mind, you may also find the voice of one or both of your parents or of other significant people in your life. You can use this practice with any voice that comes in. For now, let's look at just these two.

The child is the part of you that wants you to play and indulge in life and have more fun. It will say things like: "Oh, I really want a cookie. I should have a cookie. Can't I have a cookie? I feel so good today. I've done so much. I worked out this morning, so I can have a cookie." It's the part of you that wants to nourish you; it wants you to do fun things, wants you to take time off work, wants you to lie in bed longer in the morning and sleep in. Then we have the other part, the critic — the part of you that wants you to be driven, to succeed, to be disciplined. "No, you can't have a cookie. You're on a diet. You want to lose weight, so have a carrot. There are too many calories in that cookie. Stay away from the cookie." Or: "You need to get out of bed. There are so many things you want to do today, and you're never going to get them done unless you get out of bed." Or: "You promised yourself you'd get out of bed and exercise before work this morning. Get out of bed and get going." So the critic is the one that drives you forward. It's the taskmaster, the voice inside you that is whipping you a little so you'll do better, be your best.

Each has its place, and both are important in life. However, in any given moment only one of them is correct. The key is to use your IGS to identify which one opens you in any given moment, and then follow that one's advice. Let's take the situation where you're lying in bed in the morning, trying to decide what to do. If you don't use your IGS to make the decision, then the voice that lost the argument will keep on arguing. If you lie in bed the critic will keep right on badgering you, and if you get out of bed the child will hang around whining. However, if you open at the prospect of staying in bed, then you can quiet the critic by knowing that staying in bed is the best option at the moment. And if you open at getting out of bed, you can quiet the whining child by knowing it's the best choice at that time. With the opening comes a calm and peaceful mind.

Before I found my IGS, I felt like a slave in the middle, struggling to satisfy two masters. Now I am the master making empowering choices. With my IGS I can feel sure that the choice is right and really enjoy both voices equally. My life feels simpler and better balanced.

Everyone has their own mental version of the child and the critic. These two show up anytime you're caught in a back-and-forth thought pattern. For a better view of how they operate in you, look for a time when your mind goes back and forth. It can be about anything at all. As it is happening, slow it down and notice which voice is opening you at that moment. It may sound like this: "I don't want to get out of bed. I want to spend ten more minutes here." Notice whether your IGS opens you in response to those thoughts. If it does, then stay in bed until you feel closed in response to staying any longer. At first, the losing voice may argue. Simply go back to the sensation of opening, and in no time your mind will begin to trust that the IGS is correct, and it will stop arguing and let you really enjoy staying in bed.

Your IGS actually knows when extra time in bed is needed and when it is not appropriate. If you need to get out of the house early, which means you need to get up, it knows that. I don't know how it knows, but it does.

As you do the following practice, over time you will find you have more energy and focus. You will more fully enjoy working hard and playing hard. When you listen to the voice that opens you, things get simpler and the feeling of being disappointed in your choices goes away.

PRACTICE

Write out a description of a decision you are trying to make that has your mind going back and forth. Notice which side of the argument sounds like the child, and which sounds like the critic. Drop into your listening and find which one opens you. Choose that side of the argument, and calm the thoughts that you are not choosing to follow. Do this by letting yourself enjoy what you have chosen, knowing it is right for you.

HELPFUL HINT

It can be good to look at the thoughts you have in general and label them "child" or "critic" when possible. Even when there is no back-and-forth happening, your mind is still judging your performance and quality of life via these two personalities. Getting to know them in all situations lets you become their master much more quickly.

Urging from Your IGS

Not all the sensations you receive from your IGS are responses to your thoughts. Independent of your thoughts, the IGS gives you what I call "urgings." Say, for example, you feel the desire to take a new way home. Out of the blue, you choose a different route, and you find that amazing new park, restaurant, or bookstore that you have been looking for. Another way the IGS urges you is when you get the feeling that you simply have to call a friend, and it turns out they were just thinking about you or needed you. Or when you are about to leave the house and you feel the urge to grab a jacket, or that item you want to return to the store, or your checkbook, and it turns out to be the exact thing you needed. Or you are leaving the house, you get the urge, and you ignore it, only to find you must return later to retrieve the item you ignored when you had the urge to grab it. We all have these feelings, but we don't necessarily credit them as being anything other than coincidence.

These urgings are more than coincidences. They are important, and they must be listened to.

This is not to say that we don't have urges that are addiction related or are compulsions. The difference between these and the urgings that I've been discussing depends on whether your IGS opens or closes you, and where those urges are coming from. For instance, is the urge a habitual response to an unpleasant emotional sensation or to stress in your life? You may feel an urge to do a particular thing, such as eating sweets, drinking alcohol, or marathon TV watching, when you want to hide from pain and stress. However, if that choice is not right for you, then your IGS will close you as you do any of these things. Sometimes you may be guided to do them because you need a break. If that occurs, you will feel open while doing them and closed when you beat yourself up about them.

What I describe as the urging of your IGS feels like an opening in response to a magnetic pull, which you may or may not become aware of without some practice. It is very similar to the way you feel when you get an urge to call a friend out of the blue or you suddenly change your plans because something else occurs to you that feels better. The following example may help you understand the difference between an urging of your IGS and a habitual response.

I was preparing for a very, very long business trip. There was so much to do in a short afternoon. As I was busily accomplishing what needed to be completed, I kept getting the urge to go to my local coffee shop, Peet's. Peet's has long been a cosmic place for me, where I meet up with friends and have amazing experiences that just seem to "happen" to me. On that particular afternoon, I had no time for it. At first I discounted the urging as simply my desire to not be packing and getting the house organized for my long absence.

Quickly, I realized that my IGS was giving me stronger and more insistent messages to go to Peet's to get coffee. The funny thing is that I started getting frustrated with my IGS. You too will experience this — almost like arguing with a child. I did not even want a coffee! Fine, I decided. I would get it out of the way. Off to Peet's I went. I got my coffee and, as I was leaving, I started to close. When I checked my thoughts, I realized that I was thinking of heading home to the checklist that still needed completing before I went on my trip. When I thought about staying, sitting, and drinking my coffee, I opened! Now I was really annoyed, but I have learned that if I don't listen to my IGS, the outcome will not be as positive. So I went over to the barstools facing the window and sat down, pretty much in a huff even though I felt open. The woman next to me started chatting about what I do, and I thought, "Oh, cosmic Peet's, maybe this is why I am here." But the thought closed me.

We chatted for a few minutes, and then I saw a friend of mine who lives at least twenty miles away walking across the street and into the café. She got her coffee, and I turned around to surprise her and say hello. The woman I had just been talking to turned back to the window and her newspaper. I asked my girlfriend why she was in the area, and she unleashed a rush of excitement. She told me that she had just graduated from school and was applying for a job as a counselor at a center for abused children (she gave me the name), and that she was on her way to a very important interview. She was so inspired by the work this children's center was doing that she went to school specifically because she wanted to work at this particular place. It was a dream of hers.

The woman I had been speaking with turned around with

a shocked look on her face and said, "I'm the one who's going to be interviewing you." You can't imagine the looks on their faces. My friend got a chance to gush about her passion with absolute authenticity and excitement. The two of them began talking, and I suddenly had an urging to return home and finish my packing. As it turned out, I got everything done, made my plane on time, and got to be a part of some divine plan to bring these two together in a way they had not expected. My friend got the job.

The urgings given to you by your IGS will not always make sense, and you will not always see immediate results. Sometimes you will get an urge to take a nap, spend more time with your cat, or simply drive a different way home. Over the years I have found that miracles both great and small have come from following these precious openings.

PRACTICE

When you are uncertain about what to do next, stop and sit and drop into your listening. Wait to see where you begin to feel a pulling sensation. It may be small at first — such as the urge to go get a cup of coffee or organize something. Notice when you feel you are in or out of the flow, when things seem easier or harder. When it feels easy, flow with it, but when it becomes difficult, stop, drop into your listening, and wait until you again feel the urge to do something you desire.

Asking Direct Questions

As a rule I don't recommend that you sit and just ask questions of your IGS. Working with hundreds of clients, I have found that some people get stuck asking about everything in their lives instead of living. Your IGS is a guidance system that works best when you are living your life. Otherwise it's like sitting in your parked car just punching destinations into your GPS, yet never moving. Sure, you will get the response indicating that it knows the way, but until you actually start driving, most of the GPS features are not functioning. As you go about your day, check in and feel your IGS as you plan, organize, and deal with your life. That is how its guidance works best.

The mind often starts a zealous quest to know everything, asking: "Should I do this, or should I do that?" "Is this the right person for me?" "Is it part of my highest purpose to leave my job?" "Would this be the best area for me to live in?" Most often your IGS gives you what you need to know, as you need to know it. It knows what is the right amount of guidance and what to hold back so that you won't zoom ahead too fast and fall off track. Sometimes not enough information is available

— all the puzzle pieces have not fallen into place yet — for your IGS to give you guidance. If you can *visualize* moving down a specific path, or you *feel* yourself moving in a particular direction and wonder what it will entail, you will have clearer openings and closings than if you ask specific questions. That said, you will most likely still want to directly ask your IGS for guidance. The following is what I have found works best.

Questions versus Statements

If you are going to ask your IGS for specific information from time to time, then you need to find out *how* to ask for it. Some people are question people, and some are statement people — and some are both. I recommend testing yourself to discover which gives you a better opening response. It's simple: ask as you did in the sample practice at the beginning of the book, in the section "How to Quiet Your Mind to Feel Your IGS."

The first step is always to quiet your mind by dropping into your listening. Then focus on just one thought at a time. If this sounds easy, it is not. This practice often works only with simple things. Take a moment to identify a question you would like an answer to regarding an important area in your life, such as your career, relationship, or financial situation. Then wait as multiple thoughts rush at you at once. This happens because each of these areas has so much associated with it, including beliefs, memories, future projections, and/or fear. When you ask the question, your mind will present all the existing pros and cons or a barrage of answers of all kinds.

That's what the mind is supposed to do, right? Your IGS

is attempting to guide you in understanding your thoughts and discovering which ones are actually true. When you have multiple thoughts racing around, you are getting guidance on the bulk of them. Sometimes this can feel confusing and things can become unclear. You can ask your IGS direct questions only when you are calm and your mind is clear. If you have multiple racing thoughts, do not try to use this technique. Instead, you can do "The Frozen Mind: Changing the Channel" exercise on page 152. Or you can write down those racing thoughts and then slowly read what you wrote, noticing the response of your IGS as you read.

PRACTICE

First drop into your listening, and then ask, "Am I a question person?" Wait for a response. Next, say to yourself, "I am a statement person." Wait for a response. Then ask, "Am I both?" Which one gave you the strongest opening? You may get an opening in response to two of the three prompts. The strongest one is the one you want to listen to. You will get more consistent openings and closings if you understand what your IGS responds to most effectively: questions or statements or both.

Getting to the Bottom of Fear

When you have fearful thoughts and are closed, this means you have a desire that you are not expressing. There is a difference between fearful thoughts and your body's fight-or-flight response to a genuinely dangerous situation. When you feel fear in a truly dangerous circumstance, your brain releases adrenaline and you also feel the sensation of opening, which signals that you need to take action.

Occasionally, you can simply express at the moment what you desire and the closing sensation will ease and disappear. However, people have layer upon layer of fears that have accumulated in their bodies over the years. So it takes a bit of digging to find the actual "bottom" of the fear.

This exercise can be used anytime you are feeling a powerful fear sensation and remain closed when you think about what you desire to have happen at that moment. This means you need to "unlayer" the fear. When you get to the end of the following practice, you will have expressed all your desires in the situation and you will have released the fear.

PRACTICE

Take a piece of paper and draw a line down the center. At the top of one column, put "Fears," and at the top of the other put "Desires." Start at the top of the column labeled "Fears." Identify one of your fears and write it down. Then ask yourself: What is the worst that could happen if this thing you fear were to happen? Write down what you have identified as the worst that could happen. Then ask yourself: What is the worst that could happen if *that* thing were to occur? Keep doing this until you get to the point where you identify the absolute worst that could happen. You may need two or three sheets of paper. Often people can get to the worst within four to seven fears.

Then, starting at the bottom of the "Desires" column, directly across from the last fear, write what you desire to happen instead of that fear. Keep working up the list, stating what you desire. This will be different for every person. The bottommost desire is the desire that has been covered up over the course of many years. It is the one most important for your soul and you to desire. This exercise erases years of fears and leaves you with new perspectives on what is really important to you. See the example below.

Fears	Desires
I fear that I will not be able to pay my mortgage.	I desire to easily afford my home.
I will lose my home.	I want a stable income and to be able to care for my home.
I will be living on the street.	I always desire to have a lovely home.
No one will love me or help me.	I desire to have support and love.
I will be totally ashamed of my life.	I want to be proud of my life.
I will want to die.	I want to always be filled with a desire to live.

HELPFUL HINT

Some people feel that if they state the worst thing that could happen, it could somehow come true. If you feel closed after you state your fear, this means it is not true and is not coming into your life. If you state a worst-case scenario that you fear, and you open, then the fear will still go away, but you will know you need to take action to prevent that scenario. In all the years of doing this exercise with students, I have never had someone report that their fear overtook them and came true. What you will find is that not stating the worst-case fear, and not finding the corresponding desire, lets the scenario remain in your mental framework. This is more dangerous, and it will have you feeling more miserable than if you were to get to the bottom of your fears. Once the fear is gone, then you are free to focus on what you desire, and magical shifts will occur in your life.

Being Controlling Is Closing

Controlling behavior comes from fear. People give many justifications for being controlling. Here are a few of the reasons I often hear people give for such behavior:

- The others don't know what they are doing; they will mess things up and I will have to take the blame.
- The job won't be done the right way, and I will have to redo it myself.
- The others could hurt themselves if they try to do the job.
- My reputation is on the line, and I need to protect myself; I don't want the others to make me look bad.
- They will make themselves look bad.

The list goes on and on, but if you look at each of these statements, fear underlies each one — a fear that the speaker is not sharing with others. If the speaker were to share it, then everyone involved could participate in solving it together. When someone is being controlling, it can be difficult to address, because that person believes they have such good reasons for controlling the situation and the people around them.

Unfortunately, this creates problems and suffering for themselves and others.

To discover if you are being controlling, or whether you have a real reason to interfere in a situation, ask yourself the following four questions.

1. Is the person or team competent? Meaning, do they have the skills to do the task or activity in question?
2. Is the person or team reliable? Do they routinely accomplish what they say they will accomplish, and do they do it on time?
3. Is the person or team sincere? Meaning, are they honest and trustworthy, or do they lie or cheat?
4. Do they have the resources they need in order to do the task well? Or is there anything missing that they may need: instructions, specific people who need to be involved, or tangible items required to do the task well?

For example, let's say you ask yourself whether the person or team is sincere. If your answer is yes, and if you open as you answer that question, then, yes, you are being controlling. You have a fear, one that you need to turn into a desire and then express. Sometimes the fear may be unfounded and may relate to something from your past. If you close in response to one or more of these questions, then you are not being controlling. Instead you have legitimate concerns that need to be addressed and resolved before you proceed. Each question is outlined in the exercise below, along with directions on how to move toward a resolution in the situation or with the person. Then you can relax and trust that things will be done well.

As children we often collect controlling behaviors to try to limit our own fears or suffering. For instance, when my mom would come home from work, her mood would be determined by the condition of the house. To keep the peace, I learned to clean up the house before she came home. Later in life this led to struggles with roommates: I would try to control when they straightened up the house. If the house became messy, I would get anxious and instantly try to control their behavior.

In this situation I had to use the fears/desires practice in the previous section of the book (page 118) to uncover my biggest fear and biggest desire. I wanted the people in my home to be happy with me even if the house were messy.

This practice is amazingly effective at helping you get along with your family, your friends, and your colleagues at work. It is a cure for micromanaging a team and a cure for butting into people's lives where you don't belong. Your children, spouse, and coworkers will immediately notice a massive shift in you when you take the time to do this practice and deal with your own fear instead of trying to soothe it by controlling the world around you.

PRACTICE

When you notice that you want to micromanage a person or situation, ask these four questions about the other person(s) involved.

1. **Are they competent?** If the answer is yes and it opens you, go on to question 2. If they are not competent, then as you think of them being competent you will close. Think about what it will take to make them competent; or discuss the situation with them from the perspective that they are not competent.

2. **Are they reliable?** If the answer is yes and it opens you, then go on to question 3. If they are not reliable, then think about how they can become so. Or consider how you can set up a structure and set boundaries. Or discuss the situation with them from the perspective that they are not reliable.

3. **Are they sincere?** If the answer is yes and it opens you, go on to question 4. If this person is not sincere, then you cannot trust them. Insincerity is difficult to fix. If you are dealing with a child or family member, then you need to have a frank discussion about why you cannot trust them and to tell them they need to rebuild your trust. Use specific situations as examples when you talk to them. Have the discussion only if the prospect opens you, and discuss only topics that open you. That way you will be using your IGS to create the healthiest and most nourishing situation. If the person in question is an employee or teammate, you need to let them go or limit your contact with them, if the prospect of doing so opens you.

4. **Do they have the resources they need?** If the answer is yes and it opens you, then you can trust that this person or team has the resources. If you open in response to each of the four questions, then go work on your own fears and get to the bottom of why you feel like controlling the situation. You can use your IGS to uncover what's going on, and you can do the exercise in the "Getting to the Bottom of Fear" section (page 118). If the answer to the questions is no, and it closes you, then look at how to get the resources they need.

Reacting versus Responding

There is a very big difference between reacting to a situation and responding to it. Reacting is often based on an assumption or an immediate assessment that your mind has made based on past experience, not the actual present situation. The impulse to react often comes from an old fear, which prompts your mind to preemptively protect you. Responding to a situation entails a discerning, measured take on the situation. And it requires you to make an appropriate response based on what is currently needed.

You may be feeling or thinking that you do respond in a measured way to the world around you, or you may feel as if you always react. It can be difficult for us to realize when we are in a reactionary state, because the mind is a powerful aspect of who we are. When the mind makes an assumption about what the future holds, it can feel very real to us. The instant-protection strategies that our minds use are often what create our deepest form of suffering. These strategies include, among others: being defensive, attacking, lashing out, running, quitting, or hiding. Your IGS is there to alert you to the fact that you are reacting instead of responding to the world around you.

There are two strategies I recommend that will help you move out of reaction mode and enable you to reprogram your mind to respond instead. At first, you may not realize you've reacted instead of responding to the situation until it is over. That is perfectly okay. With strategy 1, it is more important that you notice and then go back and look at what happened in your body. Yes, the closing of your IGS will be evident there — a lump in your throat, tightness in your chest, or a rock in your solar plexus — but look for other signs of body reaction as well. Your face may feel hot, you may have a pounding in your ears, you may experience shortness of breath, a feeling behind your eyes as if you are going to cry, stomach cramping, and/or tightness in your neck, shoulders, and back. These are all possible signs that your body is going into the protective fight-or-flight mode.

Once you notice this is happening, you will begin to develop a new perspective on how to stop at that moment and use your IGS to move into response mode. Your particular physical sensations of reaction will likely show up the same way each time, and you can learn to program your mind to alert you to the reaction.

Strategy 2 is to begin programming your mind to go into response mode. The physical sensations of reaction may be with you to some degree throughout your life — they won't be as strong as before, but they'll be there nonetheless. You can remove the fight-or-flight impulse and instead notify yourself to slow down, drop into your listening, and focus on determining what the fearful thoughts are — what is causing your mind to protect you. Often, the easiest way out of the reaction experience is to admit it is happening, either to yourself or, if you can trust the person you are with, to that person. Just naming your reaction — that you feel like running, hiding, lashing out, or whatever your style of protection is — and stating that you feel like protecting yourself, will bring you some ease. Once again, this can happen because it is a true statement and your IGS will cause you to open in response, giving you clarity and comfort. Then use the fears/desires practice in the "Getting to the Bottom of Fear" section on page 118 to understand the fear you are feeling.

PRACTICE

Strategy 1 is to get in touch with your physical sensations while experiencing the protective fight-or-flight response, either during or after a reactionary situation. Examine what it feels like, so you can begin to use the sensations as an alarm in order to wake up, be present, and respond accordingly. With strategy 2, when you are in a reactionary situation, stop, drop into your listening, and look for why you are feeling the need to engage your fight-or-flight response in the situation. Admit to yourself, or to others you trust who are involved, what you feel like doing, and use the fears/desires practice to dissolve the fear and express the desire. If you use that practice often, you will no longer need the paper; you can do it in the moment and gain clarity immediately.

HELPFUL HINT

Be gentle with yourself and your mind when you find you're reacting. Your reaction mode is a safety mechanism that once worked and was important when you were a child. It is perfectly okay to feel the need to protect yourself, but now it is healthier and more productive to use your IGS as your protector.

Is This Story True?

Most of what your mind generates is based on a story. The story can be obvious at the moment, or you may have to dig for it — but it will be there. This is the way your mind makes sense of the world, and it is through story that the mind decides what to do next. Have you ever noticed your mind giving human traits to an animal or inanimate object? This is a form of story. When you get into a reactionary state, very often it is because the story your mind is making up is not true.

Let's take being late for a meeting. As we rush to the meeting, we begin to generate a wide range of thoughts and stories. "People are going to be mad at me. They are going to lose respect for me. I am going to get into trouble or possibly lose my job. I won't have time to find a good parking spot, and I'll end up getting the worst seat in the house. There is something inherently wrong with me, because I can never be on time." Or perhaps we feel defensive for having to go at the predetermined time at all. Behind all these details is a story that may or may not be true.

If the story is true, then your IGS will give you an opening feeling and you will be led to see how to fix the situation. However, if you are closed, then any attempt to fix a situation will not work, because the very foundation of what the mind is thinking is not true. One of the best ways to stop being reactionary is to check in with your IGS to see if the story behind what you are thinking is true. It is amazing how often I used to be "late" and yet ended up being the first one to arrive or had to wait for other people in the meeting room to finish what they were doing before the meeting I was there for could start. The story I generated about being late and getting into trouble and people being angry with me was completely untrue. I could have completely avoided the stress I felt while rushing to the meeting (stress = closing) if I had just checked in with my IGS to feel whether I opened or closed in response to what I was thinking.

We all have many, many stories that make up how we see the world. Since many of them were made up by our minds when we were children, they are often incorrect or don't take into account the entire picture. How could a child's mind accurately understand the world around it? When you uncover and understand your stories, it becomes easier to relax while under pressure and to be ready for the situation you are in.

PRACTICE

When you feel stressed or worried, try to see the story your mind is making up about the situation. Write it out as if it involves a fictional character telling a tale, then use your IGS to go through the story and, in each part, see if you open or close in response to it. Remember, if you open in response to the idea that someone is, for example, going to be angry with you, you will feel open, comfortable, and able to discuss it in a responsible way. You may find that you have a fictional story behind a variety of situations in your life. As you find the inaccurate story and then uncover the true story, the one that opens you, you begin to reprogram your mind with the new, updated story.

Questioning Unexamined Assumptions

What is an unexamined assumption? It is something in your mind that you don't ever question. You take for granted that it's true. Assumptions show up in our lives as boundaries, rules, and paradigms. A client of mine who is traveling the world with his wife contacted me because he was having anxiety over the fact that they were both unemployed and were spending their savings. He was trying to use his IGS to figure out where they should settle down and begin working, but nothing was opening him. His unexamined assumption was that they needed to go somewhere to work instead of working while on the road. Both of them had skills that could translate well in an online setting. By the time our call ended, he felt light, happy, and excited about researching how to begin an online business.

Even seasoned followers of their IGSs may need support to find what is not being questioned. These mental limits are the equivalents of the obsolete yellow yield signs that you don't know about.

If you cannot seem to find opening thoughts no matter how hard you try, it is time to look at your assumptions. So, how do we uncover something we are unaware of? Start by identifying the constraints in the situation, and check with your IGS to see if they really are limitations.

One of my clients had her car break down. She needed a new car but did not have money to put down on the purchase of a new one. And when she looked into a no-down-payment car loan from her bank, the payments were way out of her budget. Yet when she said, "I cannot afford to get another car," her IGS closed. We worked through the unexamined assumptions, and one was that her broken car was worth nothing. That thought closed her. So she called up a salvage yard, and they gave her nine hundred dollars for her old car. Then, in response to her opening sensation, she decided to go sit in the new car she wanted and just feel what it was like to have it. While there, she discovered she could lease the car she wanted for less than two hundred a month. Guess what the down payment was? Okay, it was a thousand dollars, but she had that, and she ended up leasing a beautiful new car. The fun part is that the new car had much better gas mileage, so she was spending almost the same monthly budgeted amount on her new car as she had on her old one, thanks to the savings on gas alone.

Here's another example of unexamined assumptions at work. When my husband and I decided to get married, we wanted to do it rather quickly because he had to go out of the country for work. We had six weeks to plan our beautiful little wedding; it was to be in August in Napa, California. I don't know if you know how busy the wedding season is between June and August. You have to book things months in advance, and it seemed impossible to find what we needed in that short amount of time. Everyone and everything was booked. Even so, I opened while looking at our timeline. One of the constraints was that the wedding needed to happen on a weekend. When I checked in, that thought closed me. So I decided to seek guidance on the idea of a weekday wedding, and I opened. We got married on a Tuesday evening. Everyone we wanted to work with was available, *and* we got discounts from everyone because it was during the week.

Common unexamined assumptions are:

- A person has to go to college to get a good job.
- It's necessary to work hard to get ahead.
- You need to stay in your home or sell it.
- You have to exercise to lose weight.
- A particular task will take a certain amount of work or time.
- It's necessary to write a business plan before you start a business.

I could go on and on, but I think you are getting it. What is keeping you from being creative with your actions and desires? Looking at your desires is another way to find your unexamined assumptions. Think of what you desire, and then look at what you think is getting in the way of your having it. Make a list of your desires and check them against your IGS.

PRACTICE

When you cannot find an opening, look at your unexamined assumptions. Inquire about the "who, what, where, when, why, and how" of the situation. Ask yourself:

- Who do you need to be involved with, talk to, or get permission from?

- What do you need to do or get to make it work?
- Where does it need to happen?
- When do you believe you need it to happen?
- Why do you feel you need it to happen?
- How does it need to happen, or how much time will it take?

Another way to find unexamined assumptions is to look at what you really wish would happen and, of course, to see if the prospect opens you. Then look at what you believe is preventing it from happening.

HELPFUL HINT

Ask a friend to listen to you discuss what is closing you, and to point out any limiting beliefs, restrictions, and self-talk. Often, another person who knows us well can effectively question us while we are thinking about a problem and feeling guidance from our IGS.

Using Your Imagination
to Receive Guidance from Your IGS

Visualizing or thinking about a scenario of what you plan to do is an effective way to receive guidance from your IGS. A great way to do this is to play out the scenario in your mind and see if you open or close. For example, you might picture yourself going to an event, calling upon a client, working on a project, or reading at home alone.

Don't make your scenarios too complex. Rather than picturing an entire event, for example, break it down and look at each part of it as a separate and complete thought: picture where the event will be held, the people involved, what you plan to wear, the food you anticipate eating at the event, and the people you expect to meet. If you bounce from thing to thing instead of isolating each item, it will be too much information to get guidance on. Keep it simple and isolate the different things you are planning. If you are not strong in visualization and are better at feeling, then just feel how you believe you are going to be in the situation, or with someone, or how you would feel doing a particular thing. Then notice the guidance you receive from your IGS. For instance, if you are going to sign a contract, picture doing it and notice the guidance. You can do this with any subject — from what you are going to wear to what you will eat, do, or see. It will help you stay in the flow as you go about your day.

PRACTICE

At various points during your day, imagine, either by feeling or by visualizing, what you are planning on doing. Then notice how your IGS responds.

Four Powerful Questions

Your IGS knows so much about you and what you are here to accomplish. It also knows what you are not to be a part of, and what is not yours to do. For some people, knowing how and when to say no is very difficult. Your IGS is wonderful at helping you set appropriate boundaries and at keeping you out of things that are really none of your business. The four powerful questions listed below will save you a great deal of time and energy when used in combination with your IGS. They will keep you from letting emotional or unpleasant situations take over your life. I recommend approaching any situation of even mild importance with these questions as a way to sift through what truly needs your attention and what does not.

You can reduce your stress and the occurrence of closing thoughts by using these four questions:

- Is this any of my business?
- Is the thought I am having truthful?

- Is there anything I need to do about this situation right now?
- Do I have all the information I need to act right now?

If you receive opening sensations in response to each of these questions, you can trust that taking action is right for you. The experience of navigating the situation with the guidance of your IGS will most likely be rewarding and fulfilling for you and those around you. If you close in response to any of these questions, then you do not need to be concerned. You can trust that either you will know when to do something, or the issue is not yours to deal with. Let's look at each of these questions in detail.

Is This Any of My Business?

This question is my favorite. I love when I ask this question and I get a closing. It means that I can go about my own business, and that the situation does not require my attention. Always ask this question about everything. You will be shocked at how rarely you receive an opening sensation telling you that it *is* your business. Chances are, you will find that when you ask this question, you close even in response to things about yourself, your family, your work, and other seemingly very personal matters. Why, you might ask? Our time is finite, and our focus so precious and our energy so limited, that it is important to put our time, focus, and energy where they matter. Each and every day, situations promise to take up these three valuable commodities. By asking this simple question, you will be able to release what is not yours to do and allow yourself to keep moving forward with what is important to you. This is a wonderful gift.

Is the Thought I Am Having Truthful?

Have you ever questioned your thoughts? Wondered how accurate they are? In an instant, our minds make conclusions about a multitude of thoughts. When that happens, off we go with an instantaneous assumption. If something *is* my business (I am usually disappointed when I find out it is), I then go to this question next. Why the word *truthful*? It is crucial to make sure that what you are thinking, and how you are thinking about it, is accurate. Here is a little story that will give you an example of what I mean.

I was at a friend's home for a party. The living room was fairly large, and from where I was sitting I could see the front door and the arriving guests. A good friend of mine walked in, and when she looked at me, she glared at me for a few seconds, did not smile, and then turned to enter the kitchen. Having experienced the horrors of being excluded in elementary school, you can guess where my mind instantly went. "What did I do wrong? Why is she angry with me?" For the next two hours, I talked with other people. My mind, however, was reeling, going over the last time my friend and I spoke, what I said, and if there was anything I could have done differently. My mind came up with a multitude of things that might have triggered this good friend's apparent anger at me, all of which were silly. Finally, after torturing myself with this process and feeling horrible, I went to find out what her problem was.

She was still in the kitchen. In fact, she had not moved since she got there. I walked toward her, and as I got closer she gave me a bright smile, which totally confused me. She grabbed my arm and pulled me next to her to whisper in my ear: "Who is the person in the blue shirt standing over in the dining room?"

I looked through the doorway and told her it was a mutual friend, to which she replied that that was who she thought it was. I looked at her like she was crazy. Then she told me that she didn't have her contacts in and had left her glasses in her other purse. She was in such a rush when her ride came that she forgot to take them. She could not see clearly more than a few feet and was memorizing the colors people were wearing so she could identify them.

She hadn't been glaring at me! She couldn't see, so she was squinting in an effort to focus. How sad it made me to think that I had wasted so much of my evening fretting. The most interesting part was that I was closed the entire time. My mind had been so fully convinced that the glare was meant for me that I hadn't realize my thoughts were causing me to close. I never even questioned my first assumption: Was it true she was angry with me? Now I try harder to remember to check my initial assumptions. You can prevent so much drama if you ask this question and trust the answer.

Is There Anything I Need to Do about This Situation Right Now?

Once you know something is your business and that what you are thinking about it is accurate, you can move on to this question. Additionally, at this point you have opened in response to your replies to the previous questions. If you haven't, don't go on to this question; it is not necessary. However, if you opened at the two previous questions, then ask yourself about the timing: Is the timing right for you to do anything? If you open in response, then you can move on to the final question. If you close, that simply means to relax and wait, because the timing is not right regarding what needs to happen next. When it is, the solution will naturally occur.

If you doubt this, drop into your listening and simply visualize knowing what to do when the time comes. Or instead, hold the thought "I will know what to do when the time comes." You don't have to picture the exact solution: just feel as if the issue has been pleasantly resolved. If you open, you can be certain that all is moving along just fine. If you cannot visualize that scene, then you can ask your IGS. I always get clear guidance if I am able to visualize or when I focus on a single thought. If you open, move on to the next question.

Do I Have All the Information I Need to Act Right Now?

The final question in the series is needed only if you have opened when asking if the situation is your business, if what you are thinking is true, and if the time to do something about the situation is now. You want to be sure you have all the information you need to find, provide, or facilitate a solution. If you ask this question and you close, slow down. The reason you've closed is that you don't have all the information you need in order to act. Enter the situation in a humble state. If you can do something there, then let others know that you don't have the answers but are there to help figure things out. What this means is that things will unfold. Usually the solution is a collaborative effort.

With these four questions, you gain insight that will help you be wise and effective. Your IGS will guide you the rest of the way, and most of the problems that create drama in your life can be avoided.

PRACTICE

When you need to clarify a situation, or you realize that resolving it will take time you feel you don't have, ask yourself the first question.

1. **Is this any of my business?** If you close, let it go and go on about your life. If you open, go on to the next question.

2. **Is the thought I am having truthful?** If you close, look at what you are thinking about the situation and determine whether it may differ from how you see it. If you open, go on to the next question.

3. **Is there anything I need to do about this situation right now?** If you close, it is not time to do anything; but the time will arise and you will know what to do next. If you open, go on to the next question.

4. **Do I have all the information I need to act right now?** If you open, do what needs to be done in the situation. If you close, stop and look at who else is a stakeholder. Ask more questions until you feel an opening sensation and can move forward in the situation.

PART THREE

TROUBLESHOOTING

Being Hijacked by Your Mind

Your mind is there to keep you safe and loved. It has very specific ideas about how to do so. If you begin to cross the boundary of what your mind thinks is safe, it can go a little crazy. It will hijack your thoughts for what it believes is your own good. This experience takes the form of obsessive or recurring thoughts that you cannot seem to stop. Often you don't even realize it is happening.

It's a bit like a broken record skipping over and over. If you don't know what a skipping record sounds like, think of a repeating thought that goes on endlessly. I call this being hijacked by the mind, and it is often fear-based. There are a few common topics that have hijacked clients of mine: fear of losing something, fear of getting into trouble, fear of making someone angry, fear that someone near and dear will be hurt, and fear that financial and health concerns will spiral out of control.

Another way to think of a mental hijacking is to say that you "go unconscious." The mind tries to predict the future, and it will create problems that seem so real a person can forget they have an IGS or to check in with it. The most important thing to know is that while your mind is hijacked, usually your IGS fully closes you in an attempt to guide you to see that what you are thinking is not true. This guidance goes unnoticed because what the mind is producing seems so real and sensible that it's difficult to become conscious of your IGS's guidance.

People often discount the incredible value of closing in response to guidance from their IGSs. Everyone prefers to open instead. Why wouldn't they? It feels more pleasant. However, in the quest to find what makes them open, people often neglect to name and notice their closings. When I am coaching a client, the conversation often goes like this:

Client: I have been having horrible anxiety all week about my mother's health and how I can't afford to take care of her if she needs me to. I can't seem to find what will open me in this situation. Can you help me find it so I know what to do?

Me: Sure, but let's start with the fact that you have been feeling, as you said, "horrible anxiety all week." That means you are closed, so the thoughts you are having are not true and are not going to happen to you.

Client: Right, they aren't true. I always forget that. Okay, so does that mean that everything I am thinking is not true?

Me: Yes. Hold that thought and let's see what happens.

Client: Everything I am thinking is not true and not going to happen. Yes, I am opening.

Me: Is your mother sick?

Client: No, my aunt is sick, and I am watching her children struggle to care for her.

Me: Have you tried holding the thought that your mother is not going to get sick and need your care?

Client: No, I just suddenly became obsessed with her getting sick and my inability to care for her.

That is hijacking. Your mind is so worried about a future that feels uncontrollable, a future where you are unhappy and life is difficult, that it cannot stop thinking about that possible future. It can be the most crazy-making experience. Most people are already having these moments all the time in life, but because worry closes them, they don't realize it is guidance. To move out of this frame of mind, you need to accept the first form of guidance you are getting and stop the urge to find an opening in order to feel better. The opening comes with the realization that the thoughts that close you are not true.

PRACTICE

At first it can feel almost impossible to realize you are being hijacked. It's like a dream that feels so real, and you believe it is real until you wake up. Even then it can take a few minutes to fully get that it was a dream. So be gentle with yourself as you learn to recognize when your mind is hijacking you. Begin to notice that it feels similar each time. Your mind will begin to imagine a future where there is a problem that will hurt you or make you unhappy. It will imagine it over and over, making you feel more and more worried, tortured, and upset. That's the best time to stop, drop into your listening, and feel your body. You will discover that you are closed. This may not mean anything when you first begin to do it, because for years your mind has believed that when you are closed it means there is danger nearby. The important thing to think and say is: "I am closed. That means what I am thinking is not true and is not going to happen." That's it. Simply relax for a while and let the energy of worry and fear dissipate. Then you can explore the situation to find what is really going on. In the case of the client I described, she opened when she stated to herself that her mother was never going to get sick and need full-time care. You can explore whether a thought is fully or only partly true once you have reclaimed your mind from the hijacking.

Asking Too Many Questions

Some people become overexcited about asking questions of their IGS in an attempt to discover everything they can about every single detail in their lives. I admit that this is partly my fault. The fastest way to get someone feeling their IGS is to have them make the statement "I do not have an Internal Guidance System" followed by "I do have an Internal Guidance System." The results may prompt them to believe that the best way to use the IGS is to ask questions. This is completely untrue.

Your IGS is leading you moment by moment through life based on what you are thinking. There is rarely a need to stop and ask questions of your IGS. In fact if you were to do so often, you would end up confused. It's better to notice the opening, closing, and neutral sensations that happen throughout your day, and then notice which thoughts prompt your IGS to give you guidance. Your IGS has so much knowledge about you, your life, and what direction to go in to create the most happiness. It knows, better than you, what you need to do to create a happy life. Because of limiting beliefs, past traumas, and fears prompted by untrue scenarios, you may not dream big enough. If you're unconsciously limiting the creativity of your thoughts, you may be uncertain about the best direction to choose.

What do I mean by that? Let's say you are opening in response to the idea that it is time to move to another location, but you are not sure where to move. As you research the neighborhoods in your area, nothing elicits more than a neutral sensation. When you start asking your IGS additional questions regarding possible areas to move to, you get closings and neutrals, but no openings. Often, at that point, people become confused and begin to second-guess the opening sensation they had about moving at all.

Most likely the issue is not that your opening sensation was false, but that asking multiple questions regarding *where* to move has sent you in the wrong direction. What if moving five hundred miles away would yield your greatest fulfillment and success? If things are not yet lined up for that move, and you will soon receive an offer — but you don't know this — then you will not get the response you're expecting. This type of thing has happened to many people, including me.

I knew I had to move — it was time to leave my apartment. And I still had no idea where I would move to. At the last moment an opportunity became available. I ended up moving to a place I had never thought of, and it was there that I met my husband. Had I not followed the advice to move, I have no idea how my IGS would have gotten us together. Your IGS cannot prompt you to open unless you are having the thoughts that will open you.

PRACTICE

When looking for direction, expand your imagination, dream bigger, look at what you would most love to have happen. Then be available for the unexpected. When holding these thoughts — not questions — notice if you are open or closed. Dreaming and visualizing, rather than direct questions, are the best ways to get the most accurate answers from your IGS.

HELPFUL HINT

A vision board is a great way to get the energy flowing so your IGS can give you direction. Get a poster board, some glue sticks, and magazines that pertain to the topic you seek direction on. It can be your career, home, relationship, family, or vacation — whatever you want more clarity on. What attracts you and inspires you to open is the direction to follow. Go through the magazines, randomly cutting out pictures, words, and ideas that let you open. Once you have done so, use a glue stick to put the cut-out images and words on the poster board in a way that feels attractive to you. It is amazing what turns up that magically matches the images and energy of the vision board you create.

The Frozen Mind: Changing the Channel

Beginning students often report finding themselves locked in a thought pattern where their minds will not let something go. This usually happens with big emotional situations in life. Unlike hijacking, which is about a fictitious future, this is a real situation in which you close. Your mind becomes obsessed with it. It could be a fight with a friend or relative, cutbacks at your job, a breakup or divorce, a custody battle, or a health issue. The issue may feel traumatic, depending on the possible outcome you face. Your mind goes into protective overdrive while attempting to solve this issue, or it has a compulsion to keep working on the problem, looking for a solution. Frequently when this happens, the IGS gives you very strong closing sensations. You might feel uncomfortable while it guides you to not think about the problem in the way that you are.

Once you know what a closing sensation means, it creates even more discomfort. You know that what you are thinking is not true, but the sensations of worry, fear, and anxiety cannot be released, since your mind is in a rut. Remember: the thoughts that close you are not true. Just hold *that* thought over and over. If your mind still will not break free of these habitual thoughts, then you must learn to change the channel. It's challenging for the mind to focus on more than a few things at a time. This is why focusing on your feet, breathing, and listening helps calm your mind. Use the same tactic on your frozen mind.

It's important that you do something you enjoy that will take your mind off the issue. Call a friend, reach out to help someone else, go to a movie, read a book, go exercise, or throw yourself into a creative activity that you love.

What seems to work best is to do something that unleashes your physical and creative energy. For me, what works is listening to high-energy music, going for a very brisk walk, or calling friends I need to catch up with. This gives my mind so much more to think about than the problem it was focused on.

PRACTICE

Make two lists to use when your mind goes into overdrive and your IGS closes you: one is a list of activities that engage you, and the other is a list of friends and family to call. Your mind may not be sufficiently creative at the moment to change the channel, so it will help to have a list of powerful actions you can take that will force it to stop ruminating on the issue. Make sure the list is filled with ideas that are physically or emotionally stimulating. Possibilities like knitting, meditating, or watching TV may not be enough to shift your mind's gears and can actually make the situation worse.

Then, the next time you are closed and caught up in repetitive thoughts, force yourself to take out the list and use it. You can even designate one friend you will call who reminds you to do this. Switching gears and using the list may sound silly, and it can be difficult to do. But once you have done the activity, you will feel so much better — clearer and more open.

Pushing to Change the Response from Your IGS

A phenomenon similar to the frozen mind is when your mind feels it has to find a response to some question or situation and begins to ask the same question over and over and over. It gets a neutral or closing sensation each time but will not accept it as the answer. Your mind can actually argue against you, by not believing the guidance you've received from your IGS. Very often, this happens when you really want something and your IGS is giving you guidance that prompts you to close. Perhaps you're making a large purchase, taking or leaving a job, deciding to leave a program or not, or making a decision about a relationship.

For example, let's say you're dating someone and you receive guidance that tells you the relationship is over. It opens you when you think about being complete with this person; but each time you go to call them, see them, or think about staying together, you get a closing sensation. Just because your IGS is guiding you to end the romantic relationship doesn't mean that, emotionally, you want that to occur. What may happen is that your mind and IGS start negotiating: "Well, what if we just sleep together?" or "We can still be friends — it's just dinner" or "Maybe I can still talk to him (or her)." The good thing about your IGS is that it's consistent. You may feel like calling the person, and then discover, as you go to dial, that you feel a closing sensation. You may phone them anyway and notice that the conversation seems to go well — for a few minutes. Then something happens. One of you says something that triggers the other, then strong words fly and the fighting begins. Finally, you end the conversation and hang up thinking, "Why didn't I listen to my IGS?"

It won't be the last time you don't listen to your IGS. But each time you discover that you can trust the closing sensation, your confidence in it will grow. Eventually you will trust it enough that you won't even pick up the phone. You'll let go of things more quickly, knowing your IGS is truly moving you toward greater fulfillment and success. This is a process that everyone goes through, so just go through it. Trust the process. The faster you realize the guidance works, the faster you will stop getting caught in this loop.

PRACTICE

When you don't like the guidance your IGS is giving you and you would like it to be different, take note. Notice how things turn out when you don't follow its guidance. You can even begin a journal or notebook so you can write down when you're unhappy with the guidance and decide not to listen to it. Over time you will begin to see a pattern in which things are more difficult or don't turn out well when you decide to do what you want instead. This is a process that takes trust, and often trust comes with time.

Not Trusting Neutral

Neutral is frustrating when you first begin working with your IGS. Neutral feels like nothing at all — and you expect to feel *something*. Remember, though, that your IGS is not a yes/no system. It's more like a compass. Neutral is part of the guidance that your IGS gives you.

Many people believe their IGS is not working or that something else is wrong. This is not the case at all. When you get a neutral response, it only means that you haven't hit upon the thought that will move you in a particular direction, that there is no guidance on the thoughts that you are having, or that you are thinking too many thoughts at once for your IGS to isolate any particular one to give you guidance on. The first two reasons are easy to understand. The third one can be a bit elusive, so I will explain that one in more detail.

If you are thinking many contradictory things at once, then your IGS will often just go to neutral while your mind calms. If you have too many choices, sending you in too many directions, and none will bring you the highest degree of happiness or success, you will get neutral guidance.

A perfect example of this is a college student who attempts to pick a major. Looking at the course catalog, the student goes through each description and finds that none bring guidance in the form of an opening or closing. The student's best response could be to choose a general course of study for a period of time and to explore a variety of subjects. The IGS's neutral response means no guidance is available for picking a major. If the student were to hold the thought that this is not the time to pick a major, they very likely would open as a result.

When you seek guidance, you will be surprised at how often there is nothing to be done at the moment. Neutral means you need to wait, use your imagination to think about things you have never thought of, or stop thinking for a while, change the channel, and come back when your mind is quieter.

PRACTICE

When you get a neutral response, start by asking if you need guidance in pinpointing the situation you are asking about. You may find that you immediately feel an opening or closing. This will affirm that your IGS is still working and that you need to either dig deeper or let it go. If you open in response to the question about needing guidance, then slow your thoughts down and daydream about what you would most like to have happen. Your desires may start the most powerful openings and closings, ending a period of neutrals. If you are still neutral after asking whether you need guidance, then let it go and know that guidance will come naturally as you go about your life.

Compulsively Reversing Questions
When in Doubt

This trouble spot, I must admit, comes from the first meditation I give people so that they can experience their IGS. Remember the statements "I do not have an Internal Guidance System" and "I do have an Internal Guidance System"? I mentioned earlier that these sometimes inspire people to ask too many questions. They also prompt people to begin reversing their questions: "Am I to go to this event tonight? Am I not to go to this event tonight?" This can work fine if you do it once. However, students get into the habit of doing this with everything, creating a habit for the mind to latch onto. Going back and forth, and back and forth, does not work and will drive you crazy. The IGS actually shuts down — it literally goes into lockdown. I cannot emphasize enough that constant back-and-forth questions are problematic when using your IGS. The issue is not your IGS but your mind. When you really doubt yourself or the answers your IGS is giving you, that doubt becomes the reason for asking questions both ways.

Think about it. What is the underlying thought being produced by your mind? Doubt. Since you have experienced the

IGS and know that it's real, what will you get from your IGS when in doubt? A closing or neutral sensation. The thoughts of doubt will cause you to close; the many conflicting thoughts racing through your mind will produce a neutral response. If you want to "tune up" your IGS, return to the original statements: "I do not have an IGS. I do have an IGS." But it's best not to do that in an attempt to prove that the guidance you are given is correct.

I have recommended to students that they visualize one situation and then visualize it going the opposite way. This can support your confidence as you move forward. It can be helpful to reverse the question once and see if you receive an opposite response. I recommend not doing this for long, though. As your trust in your IGS builds and you get used to the idea that its guidance is accurate, drop this approach. What works much better, once you've received guidance on a thought or visualization, is to ask if you just had an opening or a closing. Stating "I just received an opening" will prolong the sensation of opening.

PRACTICE

If you find yourself compulsively reversing questions, stop doing it. Instead go with the flow. When you open, follow through with action. If you cannot stop yourself from reversing your questions — sometimes our minds just do it whether we like it or not — then attempt to use the change-the-channel method, described in "The Frozen Mind: Changing the Channel" on page 152. Take control of your thoughts as best you can, or you may confuse yourself and damage your sense of trust in your IGS. As you continue to seek guidance from your IGS, this will eventually stop. You will experience so many instances when your IGS was right that you will relax more and more.

Thinking That Something Outside You Is Closing You

It breaks my heart when I hear people who have not studied the IGS, but who have simply done the beginning exercise, say, "That thing [or situation or person] closes me." When you begin to use your IGS, you find it is counterintuitive. Most people go through life believing that what makes them feel bad is what's happening outside of them. So they view things such as loneliness, job loss, people in their lives who hurt them, and not having money as things in their lives to either control or avoid. Most of the actions we take are in response to things we are afraid of, and they come from a need to control or avoid those things.

When you begin to use your IGS, you quickly learn that what makes you feel unpleasant inside is what you are thinking. Your IGS is only responding to your thoughts about things in your life. When you change your thinking about what happens on the outside, and you experience the sensation of opening, you feel better. You suddenly feel really stable, and you love that you have the power to feel good and be happy and clear regardless of what's happening around you. Your happiness comes from you. You have the power to feel pleasant and good in most any situation. When you blame the world around you for how you feel, you are giving away your power and have no real way to get your life back to the way you desire it to be. If you believe you feel unpleasant because of others, then your life can easily become unstable and even feel hopeless. However, if at times you can reconfigure how you think about a situation, and you find the pleasant sensation of opening, and then you swing into action by taking the next step necessary to continue the pleasant experience you have inside — then you truly have power. This is a skill you can use for the rest of your life, and no one can take it away. How powerful and exciting is that!

The trouble is, most people live in a world of blame. Even if they don't want to, they blame all kinds of things: the economy, their family, the person whose car hit them, the medical community, their children, their spouse, their neighbor, the government, the environment, even themselves. You name it — you can blame it. Blame very rarely opens us, and it hinders our progress. It is another equivalent of the obsolete yellow yield sign in our minds. When you clear out the blame and realize that what makes you feel unpleasant is the way you are thinking about things, you can even change your life to one that is easy, happy, and flowing.

PRACTICE

As you move through life, pay attention to the reasons your mind presents to you for feeling bad or being unhappy. It is often helpful to write down your unedited thoughts on the subject so you can see clearly what you think. Then notice what is closing you. When you feel yourself closing, it means what you are thinking is not true. Shift your perspective and try on different ways of thinking about the thing you are blaming. Maybe the person you are blaming didn't know this was going to hurt you. You could be harshly judging someone because they remind you of someone who hurt you in the past. Possibly the situation you are in now is similar to a past situation, one that did not turn out well the last time it happened. Go back to your unexamined assumptions and see if there is a "who, what, where, when, why, or how" that you need to shift. When you do find the thoughts that open you, they will alter the way you think and bring you more ease, openness, and clarity. Remember, nothing but your own thoughts can close you.

When Your IGS Appears to Be Incorrect

There will be times in your journey when your IGS appears to be wrong or to have led you down the wrong path. Often this happens because your mind made up a story about the opening or closing that you experienced. It is so very challenging for your mind not to make up stories that it is almost impossible. I once opened at the prospect of going to a business conference. My mind leaped to the conclusion that I would get a new client if I went to the conference, and that it was worth the investment to go. All of this, I opened to. While at the conference I met many wonderful people, but nothing new-business- or new-client-related happened.

My initial reaction — frustration — led to my questioning the information again. Again I opened at the thought that a new client would come from my going to the conference. Three months after the conference, I went to an event and discovered that a person I had met at the conference was there. They introduced me to one of the best clients I have ever had. So I actually did get a client from going to the conference, although indirectly. Often when we think our IGS has led us astray, it is because what we thought was going to happen was not what was actually going to happen. The timing, place, or people may have been different, and if our advance questions were not specific enough, we can end up feeling that the IGS was incorrect.

Our IGS can also appear to be wrong or off base when we quit following it after we get some guidance. We rush off to do the thing that prompted us to open, but we don't think to keep following our IGS's guidance to discover how to accomplish the task. In fact, we *were* supposed to do something, but how or when we were to do it got lost in our activity.

When you think your IGS has led you astray, look at what you thought was going to happen, and see if your IGS matches the story about it in your mind. When I looked back to when I was considering going to the conference, I realized that I had closed when I thought about meeting a new client there, but had opened at the idea of going. Since my mind could not view both as possible at the same time, it had thrown out the closing thought and had gone with the opening one.

I had a client who discovered she could open at the thought of something and the thought would be true, but the situation would be wrong. She and her husband were looking for a new home. As they looked at homes they wanted to purchase, they created a bigger and bigger list of requirements. Each home they looked at had something that they wanted in their own home, but each house was imperfect. Then she called me all excited because they had found the perfect house and were going to make an offer.

A few days later she called to let me know that their offer

had been rejected, and she wanted to know why she had opened at the prospect of this house, believing it to be perfect. I explained to her that, most likely, as they checked off the items on their must-have list, indeed everything on the list opened them. Then I asked, "Did the house itself open you?" When she thought about it that way, she realized that in fact it had not. It was farther from her mother than she wanted it to be, and it was a bit smaller than she preferred.

Two weeks later she called to tell me they had now found the house for them. It had all the qualities on the list, was big enough, and was close to her mother. Sometimes it may seem that everything is perfect, because it is. All the thoughts you are having are elements of the final path or situation. The closer you get, the more close-to-perfect options arise. It is important to be patient and go slowly — and to use your IGS all along the way, not just during your first thoughts and decisions.

Numerous people have contacted me over the years to report that they were confused because their IGS was wrong — only to call me back later and let me know that in fact they were incorrect and had not waited long enough. In each case, the circumstances actually did turn out as the person had anticipated in their vision of the outcome, but along the way their mind had jumped to the conclusion that the vision would not pan out.

PRACTICE

When your IGS appears to be wrong, there are a couple courses of action you can take. You can see if you have a story (I almost guarantee that you do) about what was supposed to happen. Write out the story and the outcome you expected, and use your IGS to see which parts are correct and which are not. The second way is to wait and see how things do turn out. You may not be able to figure out what is going to happen, because you are not supposed to. If you knew, you might jump the gun and get to the destination before the destination is ready for you.

Closing Is Just Closing

Once people understand what the closing sensation means, they often start judging themselves for being closed. Closing is not something to be concerned with. It is just closing — a form of guidance that provides you with choice. That is all! It does not mean that you are bad, wrong, or in trouble. Some of us were raised to believe that if we were wrong about something, we were *bad*. But if you make use of reason, you have figured out that it is through trial and error that we learn. *Error* is not a bad word; it is just part of our learning process.

Your IGS is providing you with feedback about whether your thoughts are the powerful ones that can get you to where you most desire to be. If you find that you are ashamed or embarrassed when you close, or you feel like hiding it or lying about it, you are not alone. Most of us who are exploring this new, powerful part of ourselves feel that way, especially if there is emotion or ego attached. Just remind yourself that closing is part of the experience — that it is a gift and a very important part of gathering information that will help you succeed. Admit as often as possible that you are closed. Start with little things, and gradually let yourself openly admit it to your friends, loved ones, and professional associates. Amazingly, such honesty generates trust, respect, and admiration.

It can look something like this: "I have been arguing that we are pricing our services too high, yet now when I think of it that way I am closed [or: "yet now I actually feel as if I am not correct"]. A part of me, however, still thinks people will not hire us because our work is too costly. Can we discuss this again?" You would be surprised by how many times I have argued for something adamantly and then suddenly had to change course when I realized I was totally closed. Then I felt embarrassed and had to force myself to change direction. The most amazing thing is that when I actually admit that this is happening, the people around me are impressed by my ability to communicate that, and their trust grows. Closing is just closing; it is what you do with the closing once you recognize it that counts.

PRACTICE

If you find that you have followed a thought that closed you, either when you're by yourself or in conversations with others, admit it right away. It may seem embarrassing, but in reality it can generate an immediate sense of relief. Your IGS will open you when you do, and you will go back to feeling confident and centered. Very often this can be the beginning of a creative solution that would otherwise not have occurred to you.

Don't Panic If You Followed the Thoughts

ollowing closing sensations does not mean you are going to be unfulfilled and unsuccessful. This is a common rationalization that comes to mind when you suddenly realize you are following an idea that closes you. Let's say you are in an argument with your partner. They did something that set your mind off in a direction that closes you. This can happen often when you are learning to access your IGS. The old patterns in your relationship still arise, until you have a chance to realize that they close you.

Here's a situation: Your partner comes home late from work and the two of you have somewhere you need to be. Your mind jumps to how many problems your partner's tardiness is going to cause. Your mind may sound something like this: "Great. Now we're going to hit traffic, and we'll miss the beginning of the event. Everyone is going to notice when we walk in the door late. We'll be seen as flaky. We don't even have time to dress properly for the event. I hate it when this happens!" Soon after, a fight with your partner ensues.

The interesting thing about this is, if all of this were true you would be open. What naturally happens when you open is that you feel calm and relaxed, so you are able to handle the situation; you are focused and easygoing. The issue does not cause a fight or tension. The tension arises when you are closed. During the fight you realize you are closed — meaning your thoughts about what is going to happen are not true.

Don't panic because you let your closing get out of control. Go back and think about the situation from the perspective that you will not be late or that actually being late will not make a difference in the slightest. (Numerous times I've shown up just when people were ready for me, or everyone was late and my tardiness did not stand out.)

Play with your thoughts and find the ones that open you. You may need to apologize to your partner and tell them you will try to check with your IGS sooner next time.

Believe me, I still have trouble with this type of thing. My mind is so great at generating the worst-case scenario, and the idea becomes so real, that I forget to notice whether I am closed or open. Don't be concerned if you, too, pursue a thought that closes you.

PRACTICE

At every moment your IGS is right there, ready to bring you back to the thoughts and path that lead toward fulfillment and success. You are always only a few opening thoughts away from being on track. It is simply a matter of looking for what opens you. Stop and state, "I am closed; that means what I am thinking is not true." Then look at the thought that is closing you. At first, it may be easiest to try to reverse how you are thinking about the situation. If you find you open when you do so, then stay with that thought. You may have to think that thought over and over a few times for it to trigger an opening. If you do not open at the reverse, then try to think of what you would prefer to have happen in the situation you have in mind. Often you will find the opening by thinking about what you desire to have happen, such as: "I desire to be on time or to not have my being late affect anything." Keep looking for ways to shift your thoughts until you open. Once you do that, you are back on track and moving toward being happy again.

Keep in Motion

Your IGS is an action-loving system — not that it won't guide you to relax when you need to, but it works most effectively when you are going about your life. At times, people contact me because they are stuck and can't decide what to do about it. What I tell them is to get moving, in any direction. Your IGS is always sending you guidance. Once you start in a direction, you will feel your IGS giving you sensations as guidance.

When you take action, you will know right away if your decision will make you happy — because you will feel open. If you feel closed, then stop and rethink the situation. Let's say you are unsure whether to call a client and offer a new service. You feel neutral and can't seem to get clear. Start visualizing the conversation and what you would say. See if you are opening or closing. You can also pick up the phone and call the client to schedule a meeting, and notice whether you open or close in response.

Pay attention to your IGS, and stay in motion as you do. This is one of the best ways to train yourself to focus on your IGS throughout the day. Your IGS will be there with you all along the way, guiding you on all the details — on the decisions you make and the ideas you have about how to accomplish what you have opened to. Or it will give you a closed signal until you listen.

By keeping in motion, you generate thoughts in the form of choices, plans, ideas, and connections to make. Imagine your IGS paying attention to the situation so it can help you make the most powerful decisions. If you cannot decide what to do, then get in motion on something! If you are thinking you need to switch careers, for example, start getting your résumé together. Look at other careers you might like to pursue. You might find that you open at the idea of writing your résumé, or perhaps you will close. As you sit down to write, either it will feel like a struggle, or you will happily hum along, enjoying the experience. It really is just that easy.

PRACTICE

If you find that you don't clearly feel or understand the guidance from your IGS, stop and choose a direction. Then move forward by thinking about how to accomplish it, what plans you need to make, and actions you need to take. As you do, notice how you feel: Are you open or closed? Keep paying attention as you stay in motion, self-correcting your approach to going about things as you feel your IGS giving you opening and closing sensations.

Your IGS Rarely Leads You Directly from Point A to Point B

Opening or closing in response to a thought about a specific event does not necessarily mean that is what is going to happen in your life. If you open at the thought of moving to a new home, you may not actually move in the end. This may sound confusing, unless you understand that your IGS is doing its best to lead you to greater fulfillment and success. *You* are sometimes what stands in the way of that happening. Its job is not to provide you with stability but to bring you to happiness. Often your IGS achieves this by taking you in one direction so you can accomplish what you need to accomplish, and then it may take you in a completely new direction.

One of my coaching clients had a dramatic experience with this. She was living on the East Coast, and her family lived on the West Coast. As we were looking for her next steps in life, she opened at the thought of moving to be near her family. At the time she was a business owner, was of retirement age, had a boyfriend, and owned a home. She was tired of working so hard and caring for all the things in her life. So she set about taking care of all the things that needed to happen so that she could move, using her IGS all along the way.

She sold all her inventory and did not renew the lease on her business location. She transformed her business into consulting work that thrilled her, and it was work that could be done anywhere she lived. She broke up with her longtime boyfriend because the relationship had become stagnant, even if comfortable. Before this, she had been unable to bring herself to hurt him by ending it. Now, however, she realized she didn't want a long-distance relationship, so it made sense to bring the relationship to an end. Her home sold so quickly that she had to rent a cute little apartment while she finished organizing everything for her big move. The apartment couldn't hold all her belongings, and since she was moving she decided to simplify by selling items she no longer wanted.

At that point it was summer, and she began calling all her old friends about spending time with them before she left. Suddenly, out of the blue she realized what opened her now was the idea of staying where she was. When she thought of moving, it closed her. As we spoke about it in the next coaching session, she had a new clarity and joy in her voice. The move to the West Coast was just a carrot at the end of a stick. If her IGS had given her a list of things she needed to do in order to be truly fulfilled in her life, it would have been overwhelming. However, one carrot accomplished everything. She still lives very happily and simply on the East Coast today.

You may start a course of study, get halfway through it, and get an opening sensation that tells you to stop the course. Another way to look at it is that you gained what you needed to learn before you finished, so you didn't need to go any further with that course of study. There are so many paths to get to where you are going. Your IGS is going to get you there as simply and painlessly as it can. As you make use of the guidance, this will get more and more comfortable for you. Remember, if you are asked to stop something, or to go in a direction different from the one that opened you in the beginning, your IGS will be there with you, sending you opening and closing sensations all along the way to support you and let you know you are still on the right path.

PRACTICE

Pay attention when you open to the idea of changing directions. Also pay attention when you close at the thought of going any further in your current direction. If you are keeping an IGS journal, write about such situations so you can go back and look at the details again later. Often it is only when you review the past and look at how things turned out in the present that you can see how perfect the guidance from your IGS was. At the moment that the change occurs, use your IGS to give you courage. Often a person will close at times like these, thinking they are making a mistake, that the course of action they thought opened them was actually wrong, or that if they change directions people will judge them. When these three issues come up, remember: closing means that what you are thinking is not true, so go back to the thought that prompted you to open, change direction, and have steady faith in it.

You Cannot Trick Your IGS

A common question I get is: "Can you trick your IGS?" The answer is no. Yes, you can play with your thoughts to get an opening or a closing. However, as I mentioned earlier, as you proceed down a path, your IGS will let you know if you are on course or not. One example of this is a woman I knew who really wanted to be with the man who had broken up with her. When she sat and imagined being back with him, she would close. So she began to imagine being in love, traveling the world in love, and moving into an amazing apartment with the man she loved. All of this opened her, but the thought of him closed her. She told me that she had tricked her IGS into opening.

What really happened was that she opened when she imagined him out of the picture. Her mind then let itself believe that what she had imagined was about him. Within a year she was in love with a different man, she was traveling with him to foreign locations, and they had moved in together. Everything she imagined that opened her had showed up in her life — along with the right person.

Your mind is a powerful tool, as is your IGS. Your deepest desires will almost always open you if they are really your authentic desires. Your IGS is already hard at work leading you to those dreams. If you have a dream that is not truly what you desire, you will close to it no matter how hard you try not to. There are people who study their IGS and believe their dream is a high-paying career, an expensive car, and a multimillion-dollar home. As they begin to build a relationship with their IGS, they may find that these things don't open them. What they want are freedom and the opportunity to travel and to pursue a passion. Those things they initially desired are what they believe they require before they can do what they are really dreaming of. This is a common mistake. Your IGS is leading you directly, in the most efficient way, to your greatest happiness and success.

PRACTICE

If you feel you have tricked your IGS into giving you the guidance you want, then try to act on that guidance. If you really want the thing or circumstance that opened you, then move forward with it and notice if you stay open. What you want may actually be what you are being guided to experience, but perhaps not with the person you imagined, or in the place or the way you visualized. Notice if you close to one part of the scene you are imagining but open to other parts. Remember, your IGS is always with you every step of the way. It will not stop giving you accurate guidance as you move forward in a particular direction or with a particular action.

Waiting on Divine Timing

As you begin to use your IGS, you start moving through your life with ease. Your IGS becomes a part of how you choose your path and balance your life. Sometimes you will get an opening that indicates you are to do something specific, or that you are to move in a particular direction, but you'll close when you try to figure out the next steps to take. When this happens, it likely means there is nothing you need to do right now or even in the near future. The world around you is lining up for you; it is getting all players and resources into the right places, so that you can then take your next step. I like to call this divine timing. It can be strange for some people to think about the world around them getting organized for what comes next. It becomes easier to believe when you watch the way your IGS guides you through your life. Timing becomes easy. You follow your IGS and it organizes life so that it's easier, with less waiting in lines and more magical coincidences.

The trouble with this is that people are often impatient and really don't like to wait when they're excited. So let's say you open at the idea that you are going to leave your job, a job that you really don't like; but then you close at the thought of leaving right away. This can be challenging. Some people get frustrated at waiting, and the frustration closes them. The thing to know is that there is a reason you have to wait. The next job is not ready for you, or you need to be employed for the next company to want to hire you, or you need a simple medical procedure and the new job's medical plan won't start covering you until three months after you begin. There is a good reason you have to wait.

Most of my clients are happy in hindsight when they listen to their IGS and flow along with divine timing. In the meanwhile, it can be very helpful to focus on what opens you. Do you need to organize your home, clean up your bookkeeping, enjoy the quiet before the busy season starts, or say good-bye to your friends? You will often have openings while you are waiting, and things that prompt you to open are what you need to focus on.

PRACTICE

Let's say you open at the thought of something you need to do or a direction you need to take, but not in response to any particular course of action. Take some time to look around at any unfinished projects you have, and which you won't be able to do when you are again in action. You can also make a list of the ways your life will soon be changing, or of what you would like to complete before the new situation happens. Then go through the list and see if you open at the thought of doing any of the things on the list. Even though it's exciting when you open to something, if you close at the prospect of taking action there is always a reason. It can be as simple as the fact that the item that prompted you to open will soon be on sale. So relax and instead be happy knowing that the situation, item, or experience is on its way!

Conclusion

Mahatma Gandhi once instructed his devotees to "be the change you wish to see in the world." His point was: don't identify the problems of the world and kvetch over the shortcomings of humanity. He advocated instead actively embodying the higher qualities of being that each of us desires to see in the people around us.

With the cultivation of your IGS, you have a tool to help you be the change you wish to see. Your IGS will help you to true yourself up to a perspective that is different and more rewarding than the habitual, reactionary one that most of us perpetually adopt. By focusing on, and following, your opening sensations, you align yourself with a perspective that is conscious, creative, and a source of new solutions from a deeper form of intelligence. By following your IGS, you'll find that it becomes easy to shift who you are and to change the way you see the world around you. The health, ease, and confidence you feel will begin to change the people and situations you encounter. When you experience openings, the change you wish to see becomes enjoyable instead of fearful or painful. You may then find miracles showing up in your life.

Every Day Sacred

The practice of using your IGS is about making every day sacred and supporting yourself as you move from fear, worry, anxiety, stress, and reaction to a state of clarity, peace, and empowerment, regardless of what is happening in your particular situation.

Your lifetime holds many different levels of purpose and destiny. One of the highest levels, I believe, comes from living with the mind-set that every day is sacred. For me, "every day is sacred" means expanding and moving in response to opening sensations as a means of service to something higher than myself. It means moving out of the fear, worry, anxiety, stress, reactivity, power plays, and problems and instead accessing the eternal sacredness in every moment.

As you practice this, at some point you will find yourself moving from stage 1 to stage 2: using your IGS. In this book, I have introduced you to the first stage, in which you notice and feel the sensations of the IGS. At some point, you will naturally move to stage 2, in which you live in the flow of opening sensations from moment to moment as a natural way of being. When you're moving from stage 1 to stage 2, you move from "Oh! I'm feeling and noticing something connected to what I am thinking" to: "There's something else going on here. On a moment-to-moment basis, I feel flowing energy coming into and going through me into the world, and it is creating peace, goodness, and balance." That flow will lead you to becoming a symbiotic part of the world around you.

Every day you will notice a growing sense of confidence that you are a part of the whole, and you will cherish your part without feeling a need to overemphasize it or deflate it. You will have become a living example of grace and compassion.

I can't tell you how many times I have picked up the phone to talk to a dear friend and realized she was already on the phone before I could even dial — because she had just called me. Or I have called her to change the time we were going to see each other, and she was about to call me to change the time, too. You may have noticed this type of instance in your life. As you move more deeply into stage 2 of your IGS, you will notice these instances happening more frequently, to the point where you are in a flow with others and life itself. What is exciting is that this way of being is available to everyone; it simply takes establishing the practice of cultivating your IGS to make being in the flow as natural as breathing.

The alternative is to stay disconnected from ourselves and focused on our imperfections and those of others. I like to think of our closings as unpleasant triggers being set off to remind us that we have a choice regarding where we focus our energy and attention.

My trigger causes your trigger, which causes a whole new level of communication that would never have occurred if we were just running around in paradise, having fun together. That trigger is exactly what we need in order to grow and evolve — to become richer, deeper, and better aligned with our highest selves, our highest truths, and our deepest joys.

"Every Day Sacred" Does Not Equal "Every Day Perfect"

Making every day sacred entails adopting a point of view and a way of being that allows your IGS to show you the jagged edges that need to be polished so that your gleaming diamond of the Self can emerge.

This practice is about bringing sacred awareness into your everyday life. It is *not* about being perfect according to your ego. It happens when you're messy and when you don't do things well. In addition, it's not about being perfectly conscious all the time; it is about being conscious when you're not perfect, and being present enough to find your opening thoughts.

Over time you will increase your level of consciousness and capacity to remain present; and as you do, you will be able to focus on opening and to move toward divine collaboration with others — collaboration that leads to the furthering of love, joy, compassion, and forgiveness. Following your thoughts that open you naturally supports you in being a part of this type of collaboration.

I believe we came out of paradise so that we can rechoose it with a greater level of appreciation and depth. Part of what we're experiencing is learning to understand what we don't want, so that we can have the integrity and perseverance to move away from pain and fear and toward creating a new form of paradise, one in which we are all conscious contributors.

Enjoying the Process

One final note: Remember to enjoy the process of learning to use your IGS. It is an amazing part of you that is so special. For me, getting to know one's IGS is the next beautiful step in the evolution of the human soul, one that is available to everyone who is living now. This new leap will allow us new levels of experience and will provide a deeper richness in our being, a path to healthier and more empowering relationships, and a greater sweetness in the intimacy we practice. This is what making "every day sacred" means.

The Internal Guidance System is playing a large role in all of this as it instructs each of us — among millions and millions of human beings — in how to accomplish our highest good and fulfill our highest potential. It is giving each of us access to a new source of wisdom and intelligence.

Through this new point of view, we also have access to a greater level of compassion — compassion for everyone in the world, including ourselves. As we work with the IGS, we learn to stop our self-critical thoughts and thoughts condemning others and ourselves. We begin to see that these thoughts create unnecessary pain. As we interrupt them more quickly and frequently, their hold on us starts to expire. We notice that we are opened by expressions of compassion and by accepting our human form, as well as by appreciating our own willingness to work toward that opening, regardless of the fears of our minds or egos.

Remember to have compassion for yourself as you move through the process, and remember that thinking thoughts that close you is the gateway to new growth and expansion of being.

You have heard many teachers tell you that the answer to your woes is learning self-mastery, being present, or following your inner truth. Absolutely do this! But this time, do so with the confidence that you have a tool — a built-in sense — that can guide you firmly and lovingly in the direction of your spiritual evolution and highest good.

Regardless of grander reasons for learning to use your IGS, what is most important is that you love your life, enjoy the journey, and live to the fullest. That is truly the gift of following your thoughts that open you. You get to have the best life, day by day.

Thank you, thank you, thank you for learning about your IGS so you can create from the thoughts that open you a fulfilled and successful life.

Appreciation

M y deep appreciation to everyone who volunteered time and energy to me and for spreading the word about the existence of the IGS. Without all of you, this work would not be where it is today. The names are too many to list, but you all know who you are and how much each of you means to me.

To my dearest friend and grandma to my son, Manju Bazzell, thank you for your unconditional love, and thanks for constantly keeping me sane with hours of compassionate conversation, keeping me humble, and saying that, yes, indeed, I am still on the right track.

To Vee Beard, Teri Bigio-Berling, and Mary Chase, thank you for getting right away how important the IGS is and for dedicating numerous hours to help support its development. To the man with the best smile in the world, Lance Freeman, thank you for doing everything that needed to be done with commitment and joy. To Christina Cochrane, thanks for your generosity and for trusting me. Thank you, Owen "Oak" Williams, for trusting me and supporting me in getting this book finished.

Thank you, Jack Canfield! Just having you out there believing in me and the IGS has been a godsend. Big thanks to the amazing Smart Soul team — Tia, Reggie, Shannon, and David — for all the enthusiasm and input you are always ready to give. And to Ruth Schwartz, a.k.a. the Wonderlady, for your big heart and for bringing all your knowledge and experience to your brilliant editing and advising me along my publishing path.

Thank you, Chris Pryor, for your friendship and brilliant web design talent. Bradley Rotter, thank you for your loyalty, for getting a kick out of all my antics, and for the twinkle in your eye. I thank my dad, Les Kloppenburg. And last but never least, to my loving husband, Eric: thanks for ambushing me at just the right moment in my life and saying the magic words.

Going Further:
IGS Programs and Coaching

The fastest way to build a successful understanding of and relationship with your IGS is through study and practice.

There are several powerful, downloadable, self-study programs that allow you to learn to use your IGS from the comfort of your home. You can also attend the live programs and work directly with me. The structure of the courses is similar to that of this book, with simple practices that are enjoyable and that enable you to continue to build your ability to use your IGS in every situation in your life.

If you would like to go deeper, do more practices, or receive mentoring in using your IGS effectively, please go to www.yourinnergps.org. There you will find many courses and training programs, as well as the opportunity to work with me personally as a coach. Please continue to practice and study your IGS. It will lead you on an amazing journey, enabling you to create your best life.

About the Author

Zen Cryar DeBrücke is an inspirational teacher and speaker. Her passion is to help people learn to use their IGS, giving them the ability to be present to the continuous guidance that is being provided moment to moment. This unique, "factory-installed" system endows a person with the ability to generate consistent, successful results in life.

A successful entrepreneur and business executive, Zen has coached hundreds of business leaders to use their IGS for success in every area of their lives. Zen is a member of the Transformational Leadership Council, which includes luminaries such as Jack Canfield, Marianne Williamson, John Gray, and Michael Beckwith. She is known for her earlier work as the CEO of The Netkitchen, an Internet strategy/consulting firm, where she spent four years creating innovative Internet campaigns and properties for *Fortune* 500 companies, including Applied Materials, IBM, Electronic Arts, and VISA. She has also contributed to Delta Airlines as the technology media expert for their in-flight radio program.

She lives in the San Francisco Bay Area on ten beautiful acres with her husband, young son, three cats, dog, and nine chickens.

For more information, contact:

Zen Cryar DeBrücke
Opening Moment Media
415-484-3663
info@yourinnergps.org
www.yourinnergps.org